Active Learning Exercises
for Research Methods
in Social Sciences

This book is dedicated to all methods students, especially the duck group.

Active Learning Exercises
for Research Methods
in Social Sciences

Beth P. Skott
University of Bridgeport

Masjo Ward
Editors

Los Angeles | London | New Delhi
Singapore | Washington DC

Los Angeles | London | New Delhi
Singapore | Washington DC

FOR INFORMATION:

SAGE Publications, Inc.
2455 Teller Road
Thousand Oaks, California 91320
E-mail: order@sagepub.com

SAGE Publications Ltd.
1 Oliver's Yard
55 City Road
London EC1Y 1SP
United Kingdom

SAGE Publications India Pvt. Ltd.
B 1/I 1 Mohan Cooperative Industrial Area
Mathura Road, New Delhi 110 044
India

SAGE Publications Asia-Pacific Pte. Ltd.
33 Pekin Street #02-01
Far East Square
Singapore 048763

Acquisitions Editor: Vicki Knight
Associate Editor: Lauren Habib
Editorial Assistant: Kalie Koscielak
Production Editor: Astrid Virding
Copy Editor: Patricia Sutton
Typesetter: C&M Digitals (P) Ltd.
Proofreader: Dennis W. Webb
Indexer: Molly Hall
Cover Designer: Candice Harman
Marketing Manager: Helen Salmon
Permissions Editor: Adele Hutchinson

Copyright © 2013 by SAGE Publications, Inc.

Printed in the United States of America

Library of Congress Cataloging-in-Publication Data

Skott, Beth P.

Active learning exercises for research methods in social sciences / Beth P. Skott, Masjo Ward.

p. cm.
Includes bibliographical references and index.

ISBN 978-1-4129-8123-1 (pbk.)

1. Social sciences—Methodology. 2. Social sciences—Research. I. Ward, Masjo. II. Title.

H62.S516 2013
300.72—dc23   2011040898

Certified Chain of Custody
Promoting Sustainable Forestry
www.sfiprogram.org
SFI-01268

SFI label applies to text stock

12 13 14 15 16 10 9 8 7 6 5 4 3 2 1

CONTENTS

TO THE STUDENTS

Hello student! You've decided to study research methods—a wise decision. Whether you are taking the first step to becoming a social science researcher or are simply curious about how social science evidence is gathered and hypotheses tested, this class has something for you. Think of research methods as your tool kit, a tool kit that can be used to unlock the secrets of human society and human interaction.

Many researchers before you have used this tool kit to explore ideas that had far reaching implications and develop theories that powerfully impact society and all of our lives. Every social science discipline, including anthropology, economics, political science, psychology, social work, and sociology, uses research methods to develop its theories and ultimately to shape our world. No doubt you've taken classes in some of these fields and know some of their theories. If so, then you are already familiar with the results of good research!

Now you may have heard that research methods is a hard class. You may be experiencing trepidation, wondering whether you'll be able to keep up, and worrying that the class won't be any fun. We say to you, throw your worries aside! If you're prepared to learn, ready to open your mind, and not afraid of a little work, we think you'll have a lot of fun and learn something great.

Why should you throw your worries aside? What guarantee can we offer? Your professor chose this text to teach you, and we think that's a great idea! This text is a collaborative effort. We have selected activities from many different professors, tried and true activities that they used in their classes to teach their students. We asked that they only send us activities that they have demonstrated to work in teaching the concepts of research methods in a hands-on, exciting, and most of all effective manner. For the first time, these activities, developed by professors to teach these concepts in different classes, in different disciplines, and at different schools, are being brought together in one place to teach you.

It gets better! Research has demonstrated (research—that's what this book is about!) that when someone does something instead of simply reading about it, they understand it better. That is why this book is solely composed of hands-on, active learning activities. It's right there in the name, *Active Learning Exercises for Research Methods in Social Sciences*. We have seen in our classes that when students participate in a relevant activity, they can quickly grasp the concepts being studied. With this book, we offer you that advantage with some of the concepts of research methods.

This book contains many different types of activities: group activities, solo activities, some that take a lot of time, and some that take less time. Each one of them is directly related to a concept of research methods, and each one can help you to unlock the secrets of research and help you on the way to becoming a great researcher. The only thing they require is participation and effort. Rote memorization is not the emphasis here—discovery and active learning is. Someone once said, Memorization is what we resort to when what we are learning makes no sense.

We agree. We know active learning is one of the best ways for you to learn, and we think you will agree.

There is so much in our society that is yet to be studied, and there always will be. Our understanding of the human condition is not perfect, nor can it be, but with research methods, we can make it just a little bit better. What we hope you can take from this class is the awareness of all that you do not know and the tools to learn more. Because while it is important to learn the discoveries of others and to understand what they have to teach us, the beauty of research methods is that we aren't teaching you what others learned, but how they learned it. Hopefully, you will take this information and go learn more.

—Beth Pamela Skott
University of Bridgeport

—Masjo Ward
University of Bridgeport

ACKNOWLEDGMENTS

There is no way we could have compiled this text alone. We are both deeply grateful for the help and assistance we received from our family, friends, and colleagues.

Our reviewers were immensely helpful. We would like to thank Steven Healey and Dave Benjamin, both of the University of Bridgeport, for their assistance as we got the proposal off the ground. Matthew T. Lee (University of Akron), Matt Huffman (University of California, Irvine), Andrew W. Martin (Ohio State University), Laura Nichols (Santa Clara University), Jennifer Schwartz (Washington State University), Jennifer McMahon-Howard (Kennesaw State University), Kimberly M. Baker (Ithaca College), Darnell J. Bradley, EdD (Cardinal Stritch University), Gary Skolits (University of Tennessee), Mitsunori Misawa, PhD (University of Georgia), Paige Tompkins (Mercer University), Daniel E. Esser (American University), John Mathiason (Syracuse University), Lachelle Norris (Tennessee Technological University), and Jason Lee Crockett (Kutztown University of Pennsylvania) all offered up their time and energy to serve as our outside reviewers. Their comments, suggestions, and input, we feel, brought the manuscript to a new level, and we are grateful for their assistance. We are also deeply grateful to Kathleen McKinney and Barbara S. Heyl, the editors of *Sociology Through Active Learning*, second edition. Their text provided the inspiration for our own, including such items as format and structure and the "Call for Submissions." Jashina Hunter and Shane Staats of the University of Bridgeport and Ilana Rashba of the University of Connecticut assisted with the organization, proofreading, and keeping us sane. We also would like to thank Jay Chosczyk for his administrative assistance.

Dr. Skott would like to thank Guljana Torikai, Dave Benjamin, and Thomas Ward for their support in this process. But mostly, she gives thanks to Darren and Emily. "There are no words, you two are everything to me."

Masjo Ward would like to thank Guljana Torikai, Ilana's dad, Jashina, and Edward. Guljana makes a great cup of coffee, Steve made a great daughter, Jashina was just great, and Edward makes a great dog.

And finally, we both are incredibly grateful to Vicki Knight for all of her help, support, and guidance through this process. Vicki, you made it more fun, more exciting, and less painful.

ABOUT THE EDITORS

Dr. Beth Pamela Skott is an assistant professor of sociology and chair of the Social Science Program at the University of Bridgeport. She received her PhD from the University of Connecticut in 2003; however, she still considers herself a Blue Hen after receiving her BA from the University of Delaware in 1994. She has been teaching Research Methods Class since Fall 2000, using numerous textbooks and teaching techniques, and this led her to develop various active learning techniques to enhance the learning process. Dr. Skott has also developed a cross-cultural teaching technique, which is in the second edition of *Active Learning Through Sociology*, a Pine Forge publication. This text inspired her to ask, why isn't there one of these for research methods? Dr. Skott lives in Norwalk, Connecticut, with her husband, daughter, and two indestructible fish.

Masjo Ward is a graduate of the University of Bridgeport with degrees in both international political economy and diplomacy and social science. He studied research methods under Dr. Skott and served as her teaching assistant for two semesters. In the fall of 2011, he began studying law at Georgetown University Law Center in Washington, D.C.

CHAPTER 1

INQUIRY AND SAMPLING

Everything must have a beginning, a middle, and an end—good research is no different. Much like a perfect day, a good relationship, or a job interview, starting a **research** paper right is crucial to its success. Often, this part of the process is challenging for researchers at all levels: *what topic to choose, where to begin, how to review the literature*, and especially *how many pages to write*! These are the questions that haunt all researchers. The activities in this chapter are designed to streamline the brainstorming and **literature review** portions of research as well as to teach proper sampling methods. These concepts form the foundation of your research.

The secret to enjoying research and succeeding at it is choosing a topic that is important to you but not too close that you cannot step back and be objective. For example, you might want to study how students balance school-work and Facebook or socializing. This topic is quite broad but could be a good launching point. However, if you decide to research why a specific employer has policies that are unfair to working mothers and your mother happens to work for this company, it might be more difficult for you to be objective.

Once you've chosen an area of research you care about, you have to narrow it down to a research question because your **research topic** and research question are two different things. It is important to pick a question that you care about, one that you'll find interesting, and one you really want to know the answer to. If you enjoy cooking, then you may want to investigate the connection between cooking and happiness or, if you're not a fan, the connection between culinary skill and obesity. With an interesting topic, the process of research and writing is more fun and ultimately more fulfilling.

Students in our classes report that one of the most complicated parts of the research process is the literature review. A literature review is just what it sounds like. It is a review of the **scholarly research** related to your topic. You might wonder how to approach all the literature that is out there (and there is a lot!), how to find the studies and papers and books most appropriate for your topic, how to discern between good sources and bad sources, and how to organize the information you do find. Knowing how to do a thorough and scholarly review of the literature pertinent to your topic is one of the most important skills the social science researcher can have. We build our research on the foundation of the research that has come before us: Without knowing what others have learned, each generation of researchers would have to reinvent their fields from scratch. We don't doubt that you could, we just think it's easier this way.

The *sampling method* you choose is very important for your research; it's how you judge the trends of a larger population while researching only a portion of it. When a survey says that 80% of Americans are Christians (don't quote us on that), the researchers didn't actually ask every single American what their religion is. They chose a representative group and asked them, and then made the assumption that this group was an accurate sampling of the larger American public and published their results. How they chose that representative group is what sampling is all about, and some activities in this chapter will help you see the benefits of different sampling methods and choose the best one for you. The goal of sampling is to capture the most accurate representation of a larger group without surveying every member of it. Without proper sampling methods, data could be obtained only in the way the census does, by talking to every member of the population—and nobody likes census workers.

The concepts introduced in this chapter all take time and effort. The good social science researcher knows that it is worth it.

Jess L. Gregory, EdD

Southern Connecticut State University

OVERVIEW

Researchers at all levels may find it difficult to narrow the focus of their research. Similarly, you might struggle with defining your topics, either including too much detail or leaving the topic too broad. This activity of *concept mapping* will help you define your research focus, identify contributing factors, and clarify the relationships among concepts.

Objectives

By the end of this activity, you will be able to

- graphically represent relevant concepts and variables, including those beyond the scope of the current investigation,
- place the idea in a greater context,
- define the variables and concepts for the investigation, and
- justify the exclusion of variables and concepts not chosen for the current investigation.

INSTRUCTIONS

Materials

This activity is best completed on a large scale. You may want large poster paper, an interactive whiteboard, or some other avenue that will allow you to display ideas, concepts, and variables on a scale large enough for you to stand back and get a view of your work from a different perspective.

Process

Once you have your materials, it is time to clearly identify your main research topic, and consider the major and minor concepts associated with this topic. You may wish to use Tables 1 and 2 as a guide to help you organize these concepts and create your **concept** map. As you add words to the concept map, keep in mind that you will not be researching all of these, so feel free to fill up the space. You may find it helpful to brainstorm with a partner or two because researchers

3

often find that they are so involved in their work that it becomes difficult to see all of the influencing factors.

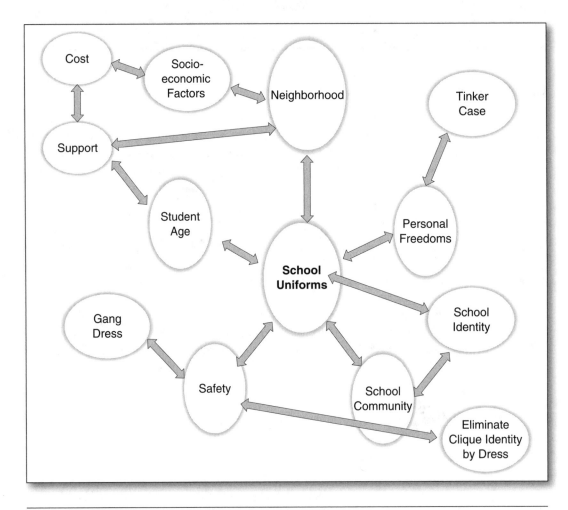

Figure 1   An Example of a Concept Map for the Factors Relating to Student Uniforms

Your concept map might resemble the one shown above in Figure 1 or might resemble a table, as in Table 2. Either one is acceptable; you should choose the one that best fits your learning style.

Once your concept map is completed (either as a map shown in Figure 1 or as a table), think about how the ideas are connected or work together. You now have terms that will inform your literature review search.

Table 1   Blank Table of Main Ideas

MAIN IDEA/CONCEPT:			
Major Ideas/Things/Concepts			
Connected Ideas/Things/Concepts			

Table 2   Table of Main Ideas for School Uniform Example

MAIN IDEA/CONCEPT: SCHOOL UNIFORMS			
Major Ideas/Things/Concepts			
Safety	Freedoms	Community	Demographics
Connected Ideas/Things/Concepts			
Gangs	Personal freedom	School/Local	Student age
Cliques/Bullying	Self-expression	School identity	Urban?
ID students	Tinker Case	Support school	Transient?
–Intruders stick out	Group vs. individual	All or some schools	Can parents afford it?
–In/out of school students identifiable		Can community afford to provide uniforms?	

The point of this project is for you to come up with a keyword list of searchable terms, which you will use to investigate the literature. However, through your reading you may find more terms to add to the concept map or draw in new connections. This will expand your keyword list. The map will continue to be modified through the research process, and that is to be expected. Once you have done some initial research, you have to make some tough decisions. You are going to have to choose a few of the pieces of the concept map and acknowledge but exclude the rest. This is to keep your project at manageable level.

GRADING

You will know that your concept map is done well when it illustrates all the relevant ideas and demonstrates the connections between them.

Your instructor will give you further details, but generally, grading for this type of project is a measure of completeness and evidence of thought. Have connections been made clear? Are concepts that should be related connected? Is the map showing different views of the central idea? Are there major omissions?

WORKSHEET A

MAIN IDEA/CONCEPT:

Major Ideas/Things/Concepts

Connected Ideas/Things/Concepts

THE LUCK OF THE IRISH: SAMPLING GREEN M&M'S

Theresa Marchant-Shapiro

Southern Connecticut State University

DESCRIPTION

In doing research, we are not always able to measure characteristics for an entire population. Frequently, we have to take a sample of individuals and measure the characteristics only for that sample. We use that sample to estimate the characteristic for the entire population. The question is, How well does a sample describe the characteristics of the population? Intuitively, we would think that the answer depends on the size of the sample proportional to the population. But our intuition is wrong. Actually, the accuracy depends on the raw number of cases in our sample.

In this exercise, you will estimate what percentage of M&M's are green by taking a sample. If our intuition was correct and we needed a certain proportion of M&M's to be accurate, we would be in trouble. There are 124 billion M&M's made each year. Even if we sampled only one hundredth of 1%, we would need to sample 12.4 million M&M's to get an accurate sample. In this activity, you will see that samples of 30, 150, and 900 are able to estimate the total percentage of green M&M's with a reasonable degree of accuracy. It is the raw number of M&M's in our sample that determines the accuracy of our estimate.

Your professor will provide you with a small sample of M&M's from which you will determine what percentage is green. You will then get into small groups in order to see that the small number of M&M's in your sample and the samples of your classmates will be fairly close together. You will then increase your sample size by pooling your results with that group of classmates. These larger samples will yield estimates that are even closer to the population. Finally, you will add all of the M&M's in the class together to get an even larger sample, which will come very close to the population percentage of greens.

The Luck of the Irish: Sampling Green M&M's	Worksheet

Your professor will provide you with a sample of M&M's.

DO NOT EAT ANY OF THEM UNTIL THE ACTIVITY IS COMPLETED.

1. Count the total number of M&M's _____

2. Count the number of green M&M's _____

3. Calculate the percent of green M&M's in your sample:

   $\frac{\text{No. Green}}{\text{No. Total}} \times 100 =$ _____% green

4. Get together with a group of 4 to 5 class members. Select a leader to add the number of greens for the entire group, the number total for the group. Then, calculate the percent green for the group.

	No. Green	No. Total
1.		
2.		
3.		
4.		
5.		

   Group No. Green =   **Group No. Total =**   **Group % Green =**

5. On the group sheet write the No. green, No. total, and % green for the individual members as well as the group. Hand the group sheet in to the professor.

	No. Green	No. Total	% Green
1.			
2.			
3.			
4.			
5.			

Group No. Green =   **Group No. Total =**   **Group % Green =**

WHAT PERCENTAGE OF THE NEWSPAPER CONSISTS OF ADVERTISEMENTS? AN EXERCISE IN UNDERSTANDING DIFFERENT SAMPLING METHODS

Jennifer Murphy

California State University, Sacramento

OVERVIEW

This exercise reviews four common sampling methods for **quantitative** data analysis (simple random, systematic, cluster, and stratified) and applies them to a specific research question: How much of a newspaper is advertisements?

In this exercise, you will work with 2 to 3 other students in a group. Your group will be assigned one of the four common sampling methods that we have discussed in class (simple random, systematic, cluster, or stratified). Using your assigned sampling method, you will pick a sample of pages in a daily newspaper and estimate the total amount of advertising in the newspaper based on your sample statistic. Be prepared to discuss your sampling method with the rest of the class and your findings. We will compare the results from different groups and discuss the strengths and weaknesses of the various sampling methods for this exercise.

OBJECTIVES

This exercise is designed to assist you in learning how to apply different sampling techniques, to give you the skills to evaluate the strengths and weaknesses of various sampling methods, and to build teamwork and communication skills.

INSTRUCTIONS

Each group will be given a full copy of a newspaper. Your instructor will also assign your group a particular sampling method that you must use for the activity. Follow the steps on this worksheet and answer the questions as you proceed through the activity.

What Percentage of the Newspaper Consists of Advertisements? An Exercise in Understanding Different Sampling Methods	**Worksheet**

What is your assigned sampling method? (simple random, systematic, cluster, or stratified)

_____

1. First, before you do anything, talk with your group members and make an educated guess of what proportion of the entire newspaper (not including the classified section) you think is made up of advertisements.

   Put your guess here (should be a %): _____

2. Next, talk with your group and figure out how to sample the newspaper with your assigned sampling method. Your total sample should consist of 10 to 15 pages, depending on your group's sampling method. A "page" is one side of the newspaper page. Describe how you will select the pages for your sample (be specific and detailed):

3. Look at each page in your sample. For each page, estimate how much advertising there is on that page (in the form of a percentage). Use standard approximate percentages, for example, 10%, 25%, 33%, 50%, 75%, 100% when estimating. For instance, if one of the pages in your sample has advertising on about one half of the page, you would record 50% for that page. Record your percentages in the table below.

Sample Page Number	Percentage of Page That Is Advertisements
MEAN %	

a. Calculate a mean percentage based on your sample (this is your sample statistic).

b. Calculate a 95% confidence interval to estimate the percentage of advertising in the entire newspaper.

4. Do you think this is the best sampling method to use for this research? Why or why not?

LEARNING HOW TO ORGANIZE
A LITERATURE REVIEW THEMATICALLY

Dr. Beth Pamela Skott

University of Bridgeport

OBJECTIVES

This project is designed to teach the analytical tools necessary for a literature review. The key here is to avoid the trap of writing one "book report" style paragraph for each scholarly article you find. Taking the research out of the picture often helps to clarify the concepts so that when we put the research back in, it is much clearer.

INSTRUCTIONS

For this exercise you are going to list all of the things you dislike about your university. These can be listed in the left column of the worksheet. The next step is to categorize your complaints into themes.

Some examples of some complaints might be as follows:

Dining room food	*Bookstore service*	*Traffic to campus*
Dealing with financial aid	*Library closes too early*	*Dorm rooms*
Not enough class variety	*Limited parking spaces*	*Classes meet too early in the morning*
Gym hours	*Dining room hours*	

As you can see here, the list of complaints could be endless, and there is no way those complaints can all be analyzed effectively. One way to handle this is to create themes. Using the example above, one theme is "Classes" (not enough class variety and classes meet too early in the morning). Other themes might be "Administration," "Facilities," or "Finances."

The problem now is that we can also come up with an endless number of themes, which does nothing to alleviate the problem above. You will find it is easiest to limit yourself to a small handful of themes. Some issues you will need to drop from your research, and that is OK. You can't be expected to cover every single angle of the issue you are studying. Three to five themes are ideal.

Think of each theme as a section of the literature review. Your collection of peer reviewed journal articles on your topic starts off much like the unorganized list of complaints about the university. You need to organize the literature in much the same way as you organized your complaints. There are several ways to organize you literature, but the key is to avoid writing a book report style review of each article. One of the easiest ways to organize your articles is to group them by theme. Keep in mind that some articles might fit several themes and some might fit only one. Don't try to fit every article to every theme. Similarly, avoid themes that fit only one article because that could put you back to the book report trap.

GRADING

This is not a graded assignment; rather, it is used solely to illustrate the concept of a literature review.

Learning How to Organize a Literature Review Thematically	Worksheet

List things from the column on the left here.

Things you dislike about college	
	Theme 1
	Theme 2
	Theme 3
	Theme 4
	Theme 5
	Theme 6
	Theme 7

CHAPTER 2

THINGS THAT VARY

At this point, you have laid the foundation of good research, investigated your topic thoroughly with an exhaustive literature review, and you've narrowed your topic down to a basic, researchable question. It's time to build on that foundation, and to build something, you have to understand how to use the tools in your tool box. This chapter goes into the basic tools of research—what variables are, how to get them from a **hypothesis**, how to break down a concept and create composite measures for it, and proper techniques for sampling.

Variables are things that vary. That means that with a variable there are always options. Some variables have more options, such as favorite color, with the options being one of an almost endless number of colors, and some have fewer options, such as gender, with the options being male and female. The exercises in this chapter will cover **independent** and **dependent variables** and how they interact with each other. Other exercises will cover the causal order of variables, which is important to understand so that the results of your research can have legitimacy. Finally, you will learn how best to measure variables without clear-cut categories through composite measures. If this is starting to make your head spin, don't worry, the activities are fun and informative and will naturally facilitate an understanding of these vital concepts.

We're getting into real "roll up your sleeves and start working territory." The tools you learn to use in this chapter and the next have a certain sweat equity. You've got to put in the legwork to learn how to use them. Hopefully, these activities can make that a more fun and interesting process, but in the end, it's up to you to take advantage of them and really own the concepts.

REVIEWING MAJOR CONCEPTS IN RESEARCH METHODS THROUGH AN EXPERIMENTAL ACTIVITY AND CLASS DISCUSSION

Madeleine A. Fugère, PhD

Eastern Connecticut State University

David M. Sianez, PhD

Central Connecticut State University

OBJECTIVES

This activity and discussion is intended to serve as a refresher for some research methods topics that are already familiar to you and to introduce some new terms and concepts as well. As part of the experimental activity, you will build a structure made of paper under different experimental conditions. Your instructor will assign you to an experimental condition. Following the experimental activity, the class discussion will include a review of such concepts as

- independent and dependent variables,
- operational definitions,
- different types of dependent variables,
- extraneous variables,
- between-subjects designs and within-subjects designs,
- one-and two-tailed hypotheses,
- **reliability** and **validity**,
- experimental versus control groups, and
- data analysis.

INSTRUCTIONS

Your instructor will guide you through the in-class exercise including assigning you to specific experimental conditions, providing specific instructions for building your structure, forming a hypothesis, collecting your data, discussing and reviewing important concepts, and analyzing your data.

To prepare for this activity, you may want to review concepts such as

- independent and dependent variables,
- operational definitions,

- quantitative and qualitative variables,
- extraneous variables,
- between-subjects designs and within-subjects designs,
- one- and two-tailed hypotheses,
- reliability and validity,
- experimental versus control groups, and
- descriptive and **inferential** statistics.

GRADING

Your instructor may grade your engagement in the class discussion, your ability to answer worksheet questions correctly, or your ability to correctly analyze the data. Consult your instructor to determine whether you should complete the student worksheet before or after the class discussion.

You will *not* be graded on your ability to build a successful structure out of paper during the experimental activity.

Reviewing Major Concepts in Research Methods Through an Experimental Activity and Class Discussion	Worksheet

Answer the following questions after engaging in the experimental activity.

1. For a variable to be a true independent variable, the researcher must _____ that variable.

2. The dependent variable(s) is (are) _____ by the researcher.

3. In the experimental activity, how was the "successful example" operationally defined?

4. What were the two major dependent variables, and how were they operationally defined?

5. Which of the two major dependent variables was quantitative, and which was qualitative?

6. What is an extraneous variable? What were some possible extraneous variables that could have influenced your performance while building your structure? What is one way to control for extraneous variables?

7. Was the independent variable in this activity manipulated between-subjects or within-subjects? Why do you think this type of design was used?

8. Formulate a hypothesis that describes what you expect the results of this activity to show. Explain the rationale behind your hypothesis. Why do you expect those results?

9. Is the hypothesis that you created above a one-tailed or a two-tailed hypothesis?

10. What is reliability? Do you expect the dependent measures used in this study to be reliable measures? Why or why not?

11. What is validity? Do you believe that the manipulation of the independent variable was a valid way to manipulate exposure to a successful example structure? Might there be an alternative way to show a successful example structure?

12. Do you believe that the dependent measures were valid measures? Can you think of alternative ways to measure the two major dependent variables?

13. In the experimental activity, which was the experimental group and which was the control group?

14. Look at the data for the experimental and control groups; how will you aggregate these data to describe the differences (or lack thereof) between conditions? Will you use different descriptive statistics to describe the two dependent measures?

15. What types of inferential statistical analyses will you use to analyze whether the independent variable impacted the two dependent variables?

NARCISSISTIC YOUTH? USING COMPOSITE MEASURES TO UNDERSTAND ENTITLEMENT

Matthew Atherton, PhD

California State University, San Marcos

OBJECTIVES

Recently, this generation of college students has come under criticism for possessing a sense of entitlement. The basic criticism is that students have an expectation that they are entitled to a comfortable lifestyle. Critics contend that this attitude does not correspond with the amount of effort students put into college or how much work they think should be required for success. Consider the following excerpts from an Associated Press article on current research:

> Today's college students are more narcissistic and self-centered than their predecessors, according to a comprehensive study by five psychologists who worry that the trend could harm personal relationships and American society.

> Twenge, the author of *Generation Me: Why Today's Young Americans Are More Confident, Assertive, Entitled—and More Miserable Than Ever Before*, said narcissists tend to lack empathy, react aggressively to criticism and favor self-promotion over helping others. The researchers traced the phenomenon back to what they called the "self-esteem movement" that emerged in the 1980s, asserting that the effort to build self-confidence had gone too far.

> "Current technology fuels the increase in narcissism," Twenge said. "By its very name, MySpace encourages attention-seeking, as does YouTube."

Lastly, consider the following quote from the book *The Dumbest Generation: How the Digital Age Stupefies Young Americans and Jeopardizes Our Future (Or, Don't Trust Anyone Under 30)*:

> An anti-intellectual outlook prevails in their leisure lives, squashing the lessons of school, and instead of producing knowledge and querulous young minds, the youth culture of American society yields an adolescent consumer enmeshed in juvenile matters and secluded from adult realities. . . . The insulated mindset of individuals who know precious little history or civics and never read a book or visit a museum is fast becoming a common shame-free condition.

While these scholars acknowledge that generational gaps and lack of understanding often lead to criticism of younger generations, they argue that this phenomenon is qualitatively different. Do you agree with these authors assessment, or do you feel that the current younger generation is no different than other generations or previous younger generations?

INSTRUCTIONS

Step 1

Briefly discuss this claim as a group. Do you feel this is an accurate generalization of the current younger generation?

Step 2

To either prove or disprove your opinion about the entitlement of the younger generation, you need to create a tool to measure the concept. For this exercise, you will be creating an **index** you can give to subjects to measure their levels of entitlement.

Create a seven item **Likert scale** that measures the concept of entitlement. Create a scale that we could use to disprove or prove the claim that your generation is "entitled."

1. Create a definition of the concept of entitlement.

2. List at least four dimensions of your **conceptualization** of entitlement.

3. Which of these dimensions are you interested in studying?

4. What are the seven items you will include in your scale?

5. What are the **ordinal** categories for your items (i.e., agree, disagree, sometimes disagree, never agree)?

6. Explain how you will code the answers to each question.

7. Describe how you will score the index (what scores indicate the presence or absence of entitlement).

GRADING

The assignment will be graded on the following criteria:

- How clearly and creatively you define your concept and consider the relevant dimensions
- How accurately your items measure your definition and chosen dimensions
- How correctly your scale meets the criteria of scale construction described in your readings

Narcissistic Youth? Using Composite Measures to Understand Entitlement	*Worksheet*

1. Create a definition of the concept of entitlement.

2. List four dimensions of your conceptualization of entitlement.

3. Which of these dimensions are you interested in studying?

4. What are the seven items you will include in your scale?

5. What are the ordinal categories for your items (i.e. agree, disagree, sometimes disagree, never agree)?

6. Explain how you will code the answers to each question to measure the amount of entitlement each answer represents.

7. How will you score the scale (e.g., what scores indicate the presence, absence, and strength of entitlement)?

LEARNING ABOUT CAUSAL ORDER THROUGH ANALYSIS OF WHETHER ADULTS HAVE CHILDREN

Edward L. Lascher, Jr.

California State University, Sacramento

OBJECTIVES

Social researchers often focus on establishing causality. We want to know if past experiences *cause* people to have certain attitudes about issues such as the death penalty, if particular attitudes *cause* individuals to support specific political candidates, if adoption of free trade practices *causes* nations to be more prosperous, if implementation of sex education programs in schools *cause* a reduction in teenage pregnancy, and so forth.

Social scientists have identified a number of principles for establishing causality. For example, in his widely used methods text,[1] Earl Babbie specifies three main criteria for determining if Variable X *causes* a change in Variable Y. (Recall that the factor causing the change is traditionally referred to as the *independent variable* and the factor being affected is traditionally referred to as the *dependent variable*.) First, Variable X must be statistically correlated with Variable Y. Second, and most critical, the score on Variable X *must precede in time the score on Variable Y.* Third, the relationship between Variables X and Y must be nonspurious, that is, not caused by some missing Variable Z. Babbie's example follows: We may see a positive statistical correlation between ice cream sales (Variable X) and drowning deaths in a geographic area (Variable Y). But that statistical correlation is very likely spurious because weather (Variable Z) strongly influences both ice cream sales and drowning. That is, people both consume more ice cream and are more vulnerable to swimming accidents when the thermometer reading pushes past 90°F.

This exercise is aimed at prompting you to think carefully about what is usually given little attention: how to best determine the causal order of a set of variables. The exercise is partly lighthearted; I would be pleased rather than offended if you laugh at some of the variables I use. However, there is a serious underlying purpose: helping you to avoid the kinds of errors in determining causal order that can get you in serious trouble in making causal claims.

INSTRUCTIONS

The worksheet asks you to stipulate the causal order of specific variables (e.g., age and income) that might affect whether adults have children. But absent greater expertise or reading, how are

---

[1] Earl Babbie, *The Practice of Social Research, 11th ed*. (Belmont, CA: Thomson Wadsworth, 2007), ch. 4. Note: other researchers may use variants of Babbie's principles, but his are common.

you to know? After all, you are students, not professional social scientists. The answer is that you need to draw on *a lot of relevant information you already have* about what factors are fixed at birth, when certain events are likely to occur in the life cycle, and so on. More specifically, Davis (1985) suggests the following helpful rules of thumb in attempting to determine if Variable X comes before Variable Y, or vice versa:

- Assume that X comes before Y if Y starts after X freezes. For instance, Barack Obama's presidency (Variable Y) cannot have caused Lehman Brothers's decision to seek bankruptcy protection (Variable X) because that decision was made in fall of 2008, and Obama assumed the presidency in early 2009.
- Assume that X comes before Y if X is an earlier step in a well-known sequence. For example, in discussing means of assessing student work, Davis notes that SAT Reasoning Test (formerly Scholastic Assessment Test) scores in high school precede college grades. Therefore, SAT scores (Variable X) might influence college grades (Variable Y), but not the reverse.
- Assume that X comes before Y if X never changes but Y sometimes changes. Consider race (Variable X) and political party identification (Variable Y). At the individual level, race should be causally prior to political party identification because one's ethnicity freezes at birth while one's party identification does not, though it may generally be stable for adults.

GRADING

Your instructor will provide grading instructions for this exercise.

Learning About Causal Order Through Analysis of Whether Adults Have Children	*Worksheet*

Worksheet Instructions

The question is about the order of factors (i.e., independent variables) that influence whether or not *at a single point in time* an individual American adult has one or more children (i.e., the dependent variable). You are to draw the most appropriate causal map, with variables early in the causal sequence on the left side, causally subsequent variables in the middle, and the dependent variable on the right side. Put the variables in boxes with lines connecting those earlier in the causal chain to those later in the causal chain, and attach a positive or negative sign to indicate whether the relationship is positive or negative. For example, if you think that Variable X is causally prior to Variable Y and also has a positive effect on that variable and that Variable Y in turn has a positive impact on whether an adult has children, you would draw the relationship as follows:

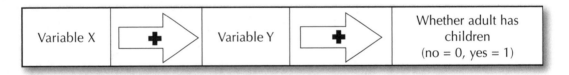

Notes: (1) You may only be able to determine with confidence that *some* variables are causally prior to *some* others. (2) You do not need to assume that *each* variable affects every other variable, only that *some* variables affect some others.

Just do the best you can with the map; there is no single "correct" diagram. The most important thing is that you think carefully about *why* one variable is causally prior to another, and be prepared to discuss your reasoning.

VARIABLES

Dependent Variable

- CHILDREN (dummy variable with 0 = no children, 1 = 1 or more children)

Independent Variables

- AGE of the adult
- INCOME
- SIBLINGS (number of adult's own siblings)
- CARED FOR SIBLINGS (dummy variable with 0 = did *not* have any responsibility for caring for siblings when growing up, 1 = had such responsibility)
- MARRIAGE (0=not married, 1 = married)
- DORA AND DIEGO (0 = never watched *Dora the Explorer* or *Go, Diego, Go* on television; 1 = has watched either or both of these television programs)
- NOISE TOLERANCE (low = little tolerance, high = very tolerant)

PAPER AIRPLANES, FLYING THROUGH VARIABLES

Jess L. Gregory, EdD
Southern Connecticut State University

OVERVIEW

This activity uses paper airplanes to examine the important concepts of independent and dependent variables.

OBJECTIVES

By the end of this activity, participants will be able to

- Distinguish between independent variables and dependent variables,
- Apply independent and dependent variables to experimental scenarios,
- Explain how independent and dependent variables can be visually represented, and
- Use independent and dependent variables in creating directional and null hypotheses.

INSTRUCTIONS

Materials

For this activity, a minimum of two identical pieces of paper will be required. There is no limit to the creativity that can be applied to this activity. You might use paperclips, scissors, staples, glue, tape, pennies, markers, and anything else that you have handy.

Process

This activity requires you to create two identical paper airplanes. They can be simple or sophisticated, but they must be identical (please see Appendix A for instructions on creating a simple paper airplane). The class will conduct two separate races to determine a winner. Before this, as a class, you need to come up with a set of criteria for determining which plane is the best. This might be based on flight time, distance, height, aerodynamics, loops, or something else. Once the class has determined the winning criteria, it is time to test your planes. Record the results in a data table (Worksheet 1) and determine a winner.

Now, think about your plane. Is there a single modification that may make it perform better in the competition? Go back to your plane's twin (the one that you have not yet flown), and make only one single modification. You might add some weight to the back or front, change the wing shape, or blow on the top of it—any single modification that you can think of to make your plane perform better. In the data table, record the modification you have made, and get ready for the second round.

Try to remember exactly how you flew your first plane and duplicate the height, angle, and force with which you launched it. The only change between this flight and your first flight should be that one modification you chose to make. Did the plane's performance improve according to the chosen measure? Record the results in the data table on Worksheets 1 and 2. Then, practice your skills in identifying independent and dependent variables to complete Worksheet 3.

GRADING

This activity is not evaluated based on paper airplane making ability; rather, it is based on the ability to identify independent and dependent variables and link them into hypotheses. There is a student practice worksheet that can help you evaluate whether you are ready for a quiz on identifying independent and dependent variables and for turning those variables into directional and null hypotheses.

Paper Airplanes, Flying Through Variables	*Worksheet 1*

Data Table

Dependent Variable	
1. How did your class decide to measure the success of your paper airplanes?	
a. What were some of the options that were not chosen? And why were they not chosen?	
2. What was the result of your first flight? (If distance/height, provide a unit or benchmark)	
a. Who won?	
b. How did their plane differ from yours?	
Independent Variable	
3. How will you modify your second plane?	
a. Why are you choosing that modification?	

Paper Airplanes, Flying Through Variables	Worksheet 2

A hypothesis links the independent and the dependent variable into an educated guess. One common format for an experimental hypothesis follows: If we modify the independent variable (3) in this way, then the dependent variable (1) will be changed this way because of this (2b/3a).

Hypothesis	
State a hypothesis for your second trial.	
Results	
1. What was the result of the second flight?	
a. Who won?	
b. How was that plane different or similar to the plane that "won" the first round?	
c. Did the data from this trial of the experiment support your hypothesis?	

Was your hypothesis supported by the data? _____

Paper Airplanes, Flying Through Variables	*Worksheet 3*

Identifying Variables and Creating Directional and Null Hypotheses

Identifying Variables	
For each of the given scenarios, identify the independent (IV) and dependent (DV) variables.	
Ex. Evelynne is trying to decide which color candy to buy for her friends; she has red, orange, purple, and blue candies. Evelynne asks 10 people what their preference is to help her decide.	IV: Color of candy. DV: Frequency selected or the number of times that color was chosen.
1/2. Pete has several types of grass seed, and he wants to know which will sprout the fastest.	1. IV: 2. DV:
3/4. Insulation has different R-values depending on its ability to prevent heat flow. Giselle has set up an experiment to see which brand of R-30 insulation keeps the heat in 100°C water best.	3. IV: 4. DV:
5/6. Alisha heard that red fades in the sun faster than blue. She purchased red and blue cloth, yo-yos, and knit hats and set them in the sun.	5. IV: 6. DV:

Creating Hypotheses

For each scenario, write a directional (H_1) and then a null (H_0) hypothesis.

Ex. Kalliope wanted to find out whether a lighter kite will fly higher than a heavier kite.	H_1: A lighter kite will fly higher than a heavier kite because there is less mass to lift. H_0: There is no difference in the height a kite will fly depending on its weight. H_0: There is no relationship between the weight of a kite and the height it will fly.
7/8. Edouard was intrigued by something he heard about slugs. He heard that a slug will shrivel up if salt is placed on it. Edouard wants to test this on five identical slugs with differing amounts of salt.	7. H_1: 8. H_0:
9/10. Matteo noticed that he only saw rainbows in the afternoon. He wondered if the time of day was important for rainbow formation. To investigate this, Matteo set up video cameras and through them watched the sky for a year.	9. H_1: 10. H_0:

Paper Airplanes, Flying Through Variables	Appendix A

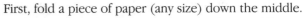

How to Make a Basic Paper Airplane

First, fold a piece of paper (any size) down the middle.

Then, fold each of the top corners toward the middle. Your paper should now look like a house shape. Take a minute to crease the folds very well. Using the back of your fingernail makes the creases very crisp.

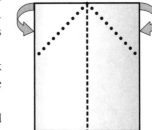

The next fold is again from the peak of the top down to the side. The outside corner will just hit the middle crease.

You can see that you have created a triangular shaped piece of paper. Fold the triangle on the middle crease that you made in the first step.

Your triangle is almost a paper airplane now.

The last step is to fold down the wings. Before you do this, take the time to really press your folds. The tighter the folds, the better your plane will look (and maybe even fly!). To create the wings, orient the new folded triangle with the fold at the bottom. Take one of the top corners (there are two, stacked one on top of the other) and fold it down toward you. You may have it just hit the bottom, or go beyond the bottom of the fold. Where you start from nose to tail is up to you as well. These choices will determine the wing size and shape. Press your fold, repeat on the other side and enjoy!

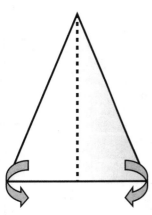

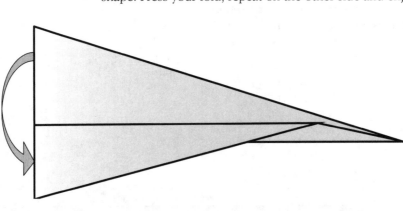

CHAPTER 3

SURVEY METHODS

The most critical part of a research project is creating well-crafted research questions. With the right questions and the right **research design** a social science researcher can unlock the secrets of society and add to the ever expanding body of sociological knowledge. The research you conduct for this class could be the seed of a project that changes the face of the social sciences forever! This chapter focuses on how to craft a good field **research question**, and how to recognize good research from bad.

Just like your overall research question, a good field research question needs to be clear, unambiguous, and clearly measure your variable(s)—these are just a few of the criteria a good field research question must meet. The reason the standards for a field research question are so high is because field research questions are tools used to discover truth about society, the same as a thermometer is a tool used to discover the truth about a person's temperature. If a thermometer is unreliable, then it's worse than useless; it could hide a fever and cause a sick person to walk around thinking she is healthy. In much the same way, conclusions based off faulty, unreliable field research questions are worse than useless. Accurate interpretations of inaccurate data can have dangerous policy implications. Because what social science researchers do is of such great importance to society, they have to take great care to craft the best possible field research questions.

This chapter provides practice in writing field research questions and clear criteria for judging the reliability and validity of field research questions. In addition to providing practice writing good questions, this chapter also offers you the opportunity to learn how to recognize good research, through a critical examination of Morgan Spurlock's *Supersize Me* and the ways in which that was and wasn't a good piece of research. Finally, this chapter offers you the opportunity to craft your own survey and plan how to sample a population within your school.

Understanding how to write the best questions to unlock your subject is a crucial skill, one that distinguishes the professional researcher. Using the activities in this chapter, you can do it!

"YOU WANT ME TO DO WHAT?" A LITTLE PRACTICE IN PROBABILITY SAMPLING AND WRITING GOOD QUESTIONS

Dr. Connie Hassett-Walker

Kean University

OVERVIEW

This is a two-part exercise that will give you some practice in both probability (cluster) sampling and writing survey questions, both of which will be useful skills in the future should you carry out an original research study. As you complete this assignment, you should refer to the chapter(s) on sampling and the chapter(s) on survey research and survey instrumentation in the course textbook.

This assignment has two parts. For Part A, you will need to randomly sample courses offered that semester and then ask the professors of those courses about administering a survey to their students. Part B of this exercise will give you some practice in survey question writing; you will write an original survey with questions that explore your research question or hypothesis. While it is easy to write bad questions, writing good questions is trickier than it initially seems.

GRADING

The following things must be turned in for this assignment (100 points total):

(a) Your answers to Part A questions number 2, 3, 6, 8, and 9 (6 points each; total of 30 points)

(b) The unique random number list you generated from Randomizer.org (10 points)

(c) Your numbered list of courses (10 points)

(d) The 10 questions you will write about family violence, family drug/alcohol use, or relationship infidelity (from Part B) (5 points per question; total of 50 points)

"You Want Me to Do What?" A Little Practice in Probability Sampling and Writing Good Questions	*Worksheet*

Part A (50 points)

For this part, you will be sampling from the courses offered at your institution. You can get this information from the course registration packet available either at your institution or through your professor.

To begin, starting at the top of the page, number each course in the order they appear (e.g., 1, 2, 3, 4). Note that the total number of potential courses to survey will be specific to your institution.

Assume there are 30 students per class. You need a sample of $N = 150$ students. However, not all professors will respond to your request to survey their class. How many courses do you want to survey to get a sample of 150? _____.

On the Internet, go to www.randomizer.org.

Click on the "Use the randomizer form" link.

Do the following:

(a) How many sets of numbers do you want to generate? **1**

(b) How many numbers per set? _____ (Here, list the total number of potential courses you could sample. See your answer to No. 2, above.)

(c) Number range from 1 to _____ (Here, list the total number of potential courses you could sample. See your answer to No. 2, above.)

(d) Do you wish each number to be unique? **Yes**

(e) Do you wish to sort numbers that are generated? **No**

(f) How do you wish to view your random numbers? **Place numbers off**

(g) Then click "Randomize now"

A screen should pop up that will show a random list of numbers, such as: **42**, 79, 60, 36, 29, 67, 2, 14, 16, 56, and so on. Going according to the randomly sampled courses in this hypothetical example, the first course in which the students would be surveyed (pending the professor's okay) would be course number **42**, Bio_2043, Introduction to Cell Biology (for instance).

PRINT OUT THE LIST OF RANDOM NUMBERS. You'll need to submit it as part of your homework.

1. **Answer the following:** What's the name and course number of the first (1st) class you'll try to survey? (*Hint:* In the randomly generated list of numbers, the first random number corresponds with what course on the course list?) _____

2. **Answer the following:** What's the name and course number of the fifth (5th) class you'll try to survey? _____

Part B (50 points)

Pick <u>one</u> of the following topic areas: (a) family-of-origin violence; (b) family-of-origin drug and alcohol use; or (c) infidelity in a relationship.

1. <u>25 points</u>: Write five sensitive questions to ask your fellow students, which pertain to your topic area. A sensitive question asks people directly about their experiences or behavior. For instance, if you were doing a survey on adolescent bullying, a sensitive question would be to ask, "<u>Were you ever bullied?</u>" or "<u>How frequently were you bullied?</u>" or "<u>Did you bully others?</u>" You might also ask a question about <u>how students were bullied</u> or <u>how they bullied others</u> (e.g., physically, verbally, excluded from friendships, a combination of bullying behaviors).

2. <u>25 points</u>: Write five nonsensitive, perception-type questions to ask your fellow students, which pertain to your topic area. For instance (again using the bullying topic area), "On a scale of 1 to 5, how strongly do you agree or disagree with the following statement: <u>Being bullied is a normal part of growing up.</u>" (1 = strongly agree, 5 = strongly disagree). **The idea is to write questions that <u>don't</u> ask survey respondents about their behavior or experiences.** (Questions like that would need prior approval from the university's Institutional Review Board (IRB), which you won't be able to get for your research study next semester.) Perception-type questions do not require prior IRB approval, and don't ask survey respondents about their behavior or experiences. (Refer also to the chapter on research ethics in your course textbook.)

As you write your nonsensitive and perception-type questions, be mindful of **not writing double-barreled questions**. (See also the chapter on survey design in your course textbook.) For instance, if a question asks about the respondent father's alcohol and drug use and a survey respondent answers *yes*, then to what are they answering *yes*? The alcohol use? The drug use? These should be separate questions.

DON'T EAT THE FRIES: USING A DOCUMENTARY ON MCDONALDS TO ENHANCE SCIENTIFIC LITERACY

Amy Cass

California State University, Fullerton

OVERVIEW

To better understand research methods, you will view the documentary *Super Size Me*, by Morgan Spurlock and explore the ways in which it is and is not credible scholarship. The purpose of this activity is to apply concepts learned in class to material displayed in everyday life. By drawing your own conclusions about the real world, you will learn the practical application of quantitative and critical thinking skills, ultimately becoming more sophisticated consumers of knowledge.

INSTRUCTIONS

1. Review the questions from the "Don't Eat the Fries" worksheet. Be sure you are familiar with all the concepts presented in the exercise.

2. Watch the film in its entirety and respond to each of the questions on the worksheet.

3. Turn the completed worksheet into the instructor at the end of class.

GRADING

You must demonstrate a good faith effort to complete each question on the worksheet. Your grade will likely be impacted by how thoroughly and accurately you complete the assignment, but check with your instructor for specific details on how this exercise will be graded in your course.

Don't Eat the Fries: Using a Documentary on McDonalds to Enhance Scientific Literacy	Worksheet

Directions: Apply classroom material to answer each of the following questions. You may use additional paper as necessary.

1. Identify the classification of this work (scientific discipline; level of explanation).

    _____

    _____

2. Identify Spurlock's research question.

    _____

    _____

3. Identify the research design of this project (quantitative/qualitative; random/convenience; cross sectional/longitudinal).

    _____

    _____

4. Identify the hypothesis/es Spurlock is testing.

    _____

    _____

5. Identify the independent and dependent variables in this project.

    _____

    _____

6. How does Spurlock measure/operationalize the independent and dependent variables?

    _____

    _____

7. What types of relationships exist between the variables in this project (positive/negative; direct/indirect)?

   _____

   _____

8. What control variables does Spurlock include in this study? What others do you feel he could have included?

   _____

   _____

9. Does Spurlock have a time order issue with his experiment? Explain.

   _____

   _____

10. Do Spurlock's arguments in this piece meet the criteria of logical consistency, testability, and parsimony? Explain.

    _____

    _____

11. Are Spurlock's findings generalizable to a larger population? Why or why not?

    _____

    _____

12. Document at least <u>three</u> instances where statistical information was displayed. Where did these numbers come from? Were they believable or trustworthy?

    _____

    _____

13. Identify an instance in which Spurlock glamorized an **outlier** in his project. What are the implications of this?

    _____

    _____

14. Identify <u>three</u> instances where Spurlock violated standards of research ethics.

   _____

   _____

15. If you sought to answer the same research question as Morgan Spurlock, then what <u>four</u> things would you do to improve the credibility of the study and your findings?

   _____

   _____

16. Should findings from Spurlock's study (or your own) be used to modify law? Explain your opinion on judicial activism versus judicial restraint.

   _____

   _____

SCHOOL SURVEY ACTIVITY

Meridith Pease Selden, PhD

Wilkes University

OVERVIEW

When you began your search for the perfect university, what was important to you? The academics? The atmosphere? The location? Every year, thousands of high school students struggle with selecting a university. There are companies that have capitalized on the uncertainty students face by publishing "tell-all" and "off the record" fact books about most schools. In many of the books, universities receive a grade in areas such as academics, diversity, and athletics. In addition to a grade, there are often numerous quotes collected by the editor (typically a student) that are representative (presumably) of actual students.

What most of the books are lacking is appropriate survey methodology. By looking at the book, it is impossible to answer basic critical research methods questions—for example, How were the data collected? What kind of sampling was conducted? How many people responded? How many did not respond? Was the data collection anonymous?

INSTRUCTIONS

For this project, you will be creating a minibook (or a recruitment pamphlet) about your university. The purpose of the book or pamphlet is to provide a relatively unbiased look at your university for people considering attending and/or new students who don't yet know that much about the school. This is your chance to sing the praises (or fail to sing the praises) of your university and show your personality. Humor is encouraged! You will not be graded on how you present your university in the book or pamphlet (e.g., it is OK if you don't strongly encourage every potential student to enroll), but you will be graded on your ability to present a realistic look at your university.

You can select any five questions from the attached survey that interest you (or you might even create your own survey questions). So if you are an athlete and think the athletic department is the most important thing about your university, then discuss that. A word of caution, however: All opinions about your university must be backed up with facts (i.e., numbers!).

As with any data collection techniques, the way the data for the book or pamphlet are collected will not be perfect. In your book or pamphlet you will need to address the strengths and weaknesses of the data collection process as well as discuss any possible biases that exist. In addition to discussing how the data were collected, you will need to thoroughly describe the sample. (HINT: You have demographic questions to help with this.)

To complete this assignment, you will need to draw on a number of topics discussed in class. Specifically, you are expected to apply the concepts related to types of data (see the "Types of Data" worksheet for more information), sampling (see the "Sampling" worksheet for more information), and validity (see the "Validity" worksheet for more information). Pay close attention to the information discussed on each worksheet and try to incorporate as much information from the school survey questions as possible. You will also find a handy Statistical Package for the Social Sciences (SPSS) tutorial if you feel your skills need polishing,

School Survey			
Coding Manual			
Demographics			
age	Q1	V1	How old (in years) are you?
work	Q3	V2	Are you working? 1 = Yes, Full-Time 2 = Yes, Part-Time 3 = No
gender	Q4	V3	What is your gender? 1 = Male 2 = Female
status	Q5	V4	Student Status 1 = Full-Time 2 = Part-Time
residence	Q6	V5	What is your current residence as a student? 1 = On Campus 2 = Off Campus
year	Q7	V6	What year are you in school? 1 = Freshman 2 = Sophomore 3 = Junior 4 = Senior
ss major	Q8	V7	Are you a social science major? 1 = Yes 2 = No
sport	Q9	V8	Are you a member of an intercollegiate sport? 1 = Yes 2 = No
siblings	Q10	V9	How many siblings do you have?
pets	Q11	V10	How many pets do you have?
school	Q12	V11	Do you like school? 1 = Yes 2 = No 3 = Not Sure
miles	Q13	V12	Approximately how many miles from campus did you grow up? 1 = 0 to 20 miles 2 = 21 to 40 miles 3 = 41 to 60 miles 4 = 61 to 80 miles 5 = 81 to 100 miles 6 = More than 100 miles

School Survey			
prof_approachable	Q1	V13	The professors here are approachable. 1 = Strongly Disagree 2 = Disagree 3 = Neither Disagree Nor Agree 4 = Agree 5 = Strongly Agree 6 = NA
prof_fair	Q2	V14	The professors here are fair. 1 = Strongly Disagree 2 = Disagree 3 = Neither Disagree Nor Agree 4 = Agree 5 = Strongly Agree 6 = NA
workload	Q3	V15	The workload here is reasonable. 1 = Strongly Disagree 2 = Disagree 3 = Neither Disagree Nor Agree 4 = Agree 5 = Strongly Agree 6 = NA
safe_WB	Q4	V16	The area around the campus is safe. 1 = Strongly Disagree 2 = Disagree 3 = Neither Disagree Nor Agree 4 = Agree 5 = Strongly Agree 6 = NA
safe_campus	Q5	V17	The campus is safe. 1 = Strongly Disagree 2 = Disagree 3 = Neither Disagree Nor Agree 4 = Agree 5 = Strongly Agree 6 = NA
to_do	Q6	V18	There's not much to do around campus. 1 = Strongly Disagree 2 = Disagree 3 = Neither Disagree Nor Agree 4 = Agree 5 = Strongly Agree 6 = NA

computer	Q7	V19	Every student needs a personal computer. 1 = Strongly Disagree 2 = Disagree 3 = Neither Disagree Nor Agree 4 = Agree 5 = Strongly Agree 6 = NA
computer_lab	Q8	V20	The computer labs on campus are adequate. 1 = Strongly Disagree 2 = Disagree 3 = Neither Disagree Nor Agree 4 = Agree 5 = Strongly Agree 6 = NA
food_good	Q9	V21	The food in the dining hall is good. 1 = Strongly Disagree 2 = Disagree 3 = Neither Disagree Nor Agree 4 = Agree 5 = Strongly Agree 6 = NA
food_variety	Q10	V22	The food in the dining hall lacks variety. 1 = Strongly Disagree 2 = Disagree 3 = Neither Disagree Nor Agree 4 = Agree 5 = Strongly Agree 6 = NA
dorms	Q11	V23	The dorms are nice. 1 = Strongly Disagree 2 = Disagree 3 = Neither Disagree Nor Agree 4 = Agree 5 = Strongly Agree 6 = NA
strive_diversity	Q12	V24	This is a campus that strives for diversity. 1 = Strongly Disagree 2 = Disagree 3 = Neither Disagree Nor Agree 4 = Agree 5 = Strongly Agree 6 = NA

not_diverse	Q13	V25	The student population is not very diverse. 1 = Strongly Disagree 2 = Disagree 3 = Neither Disagree Nor Agree 4 = Agree 5 = Strongly Agree 6 = NA
sports	Q14	V26	There is a good sports program here. 1 = Strongly Disagree 2 = Disagree 3 = Neither Disagree Nor Agree 4 = Agree 5 = Strongly Agree 6 = NA
student_sat	Q15	V27	How satisfied are you with your experience as a student? 1 = Very Dissatisfied 2 = Dissatisfied 3 = Neither Dissatisfied Nor Satisfied 4 = Satisfied 5 = Very Satisfied
graduate	Q16	V28	Do you intend to stay and graduate from here? 1 = Yes 2 = No 3 = Not Sure
school_sat	Q17	V29	How satisfied are you here? 1 = Very Dissatisfied 2 = Dissatisfied 3 = Neither Dissatisfied Nor Satisfied 4 = Satisfied 5 = Very Satisfied
Rec_Freshman	Q18	V30	I would recommend this university to an incoming freshman. 1 = Strongly Disagree 2 = Disagree 3 = Neither Disagree Nor Agree 4 = Agree 5 = Strongly Agree 6 = NA
Rec_Transfer	Q19	V31	I would recommend this university to a transfer student. 1 = Strongly Disagree 2 = Disagree 3 = Neither Disagree Nor Agree 4 = Agree 5 = Strongly Agree 6 = NA

How to Enter **Data in SPSS**

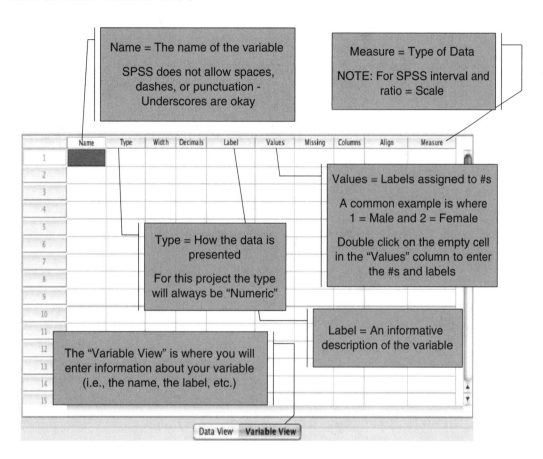

Name = The name of the variable

SPSS does not allow spaces, dashes, or punctuation - Underscores are okay

Measure = Type of Data

NOTE: For SPSS interval and ratio = Scale

Values = Labels assigned to #s

A common example is where 1 = Male and 2 = Female

Double click on the empty cell in the "Values" column to enter the #s and labels

Type = How the data is presented

For this project the type will always be "Numeric"

Label = An informative description of the variable

The "Variable View" is where you will enter information about your variable (i.e., the name, the label, etc.)

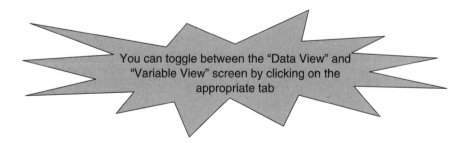

You can toggle between the "Data View" and "Variable View" screen by clicking on the appropriate tab

How to Enter Missing Values

For the School survey you will need to specify the "NA" response as a missing value (otherwise, SPSS will include it in all the calculations). Here is how you define values as missing:

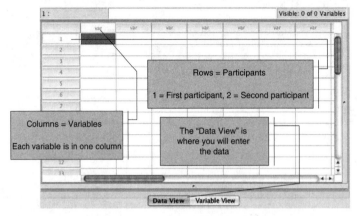

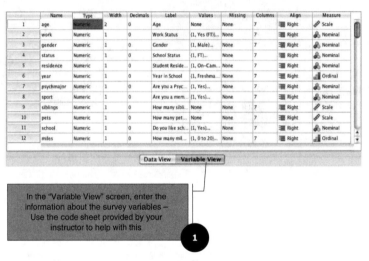

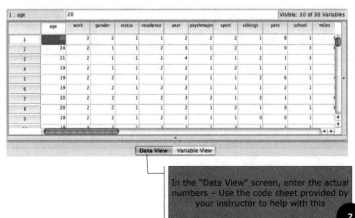

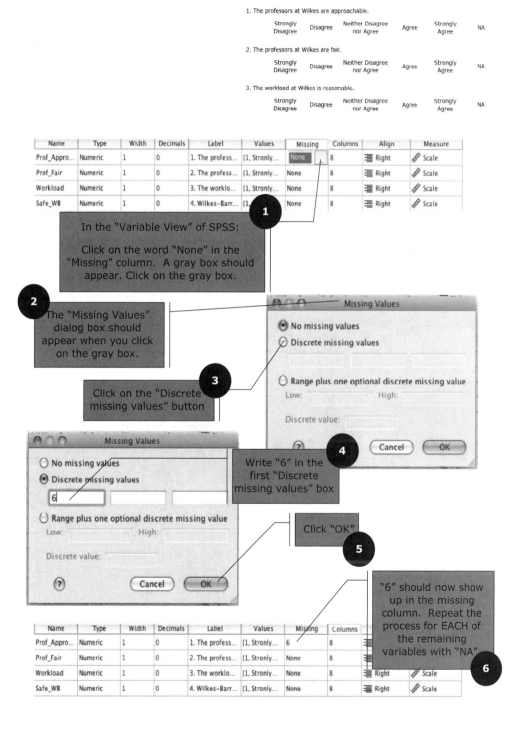

1. The professors at Wilkes are approachable.

| Strongly Disagree | Disagree | Neither Disagree nor Agree | Agree | Strongly Agree | NA |

2. The professors at Wilkes are fair.

| Strongly Disagree | Disagree | Neither Disagree nor Agree | Agree | Strongly Agree | NA |

3. The workload at Wilkes is reasonable.

| Strongly Disagree | Disagree | Neither Disagree nor Agree | Agree | Strongly Agree | NA |

Name	Type	Width	Decimals	Label	Values	Missing	Columns	Align	Measure
Prof_Appro...	Numeric	1	0	1. The profess...	{1, Stronly...	None	8	Right	Scale
Prof_Fair	Numeric	1	0	2. The profess...	{1, Stronly...	None	8	Right	Scale
Workload	Numeric	1	0	3. The worklo...	{1, Stronly...	None	8	Right	Scale
Safe_WB	Numeric	1	0	4. Wilkes–Barr...	{1,	None	8	Right	Scale

1 In the "Variable View" of SPSS:

Click on the word "None" in the "Missing" column. A gray box should appear. Click on the gray box.

2 The "Missing Values" dialog box should appear when you click on the gray box.

3 Click on the "Discrete missing values" button

Missing Values

◉ No missing values
◎ Discrete missing values

◎ Range plus one optional discrete missing value
Low: High:

Discrete value:

Cancel   OK

4 Write "6" in the first "Discrete missing values" box

Missing Values

◎ No missing values
◉ Discrete missing values

6

◎ Range plus one optional discrete missing value
Low: High:

Discrete value:

Cancel   OK

5 Click "OK"

6 "6" should now show up in the missing column. Repeat the process for EACH of the remaining variables with "NA"

Name	Type	Width	Decimals	Label	Values	Missing	Columns	Align	Measure
Prof_Appro...	Numeric	1	0	1. The profess...	{1, Stronly...	6	8		
Prof_Fair	Numeric	1	0	2. The profess...	{1, Stronly...	None	8		
Workload	Numeric	1	0	3. The worklo...	{1, Stronly...	None	8	Right	Scale
Safe_WB	Numeric	1	0	4. Wilkes–Barr...	{1, Stronly...	None	8	Right	Scale

School Survey Activity	**Survey**

The following questions are designed to assess your **feelings about your university**. Feel free to answer truthfully. The answers you provide will not be used to evaluate your performance in class.

Please circle the appropriate response for each of the following items.

1. The professors here are approachable.					
Strongly Disagree	Disagree	Neither Disagree nor Agree	Agree	Strongly Agree	NA

2. The professors here are fair.					
Strongly Disagree	Disagree	Neither Disagree nor Agree	Agree	Strongly Agree	NA

3. The workload here is reasonable.					
Strongly Disagree	Disagree	Neither Disagree nor Agree	Agree	Strongly Agree	NA

4. The area around campus is safe.					
Strongly Disagree	Disagree	Neither Disagree nor Agree	Agree	Strongly Agree	NA

5. The campus is safe.					
Strongly Disagree	Disagree	Neither Disagree nor Agree	Agree	Strongly Agree	NA

6. There's not much to do around campus.					
Strongly Disagree	Disagree	Neither Disagree nor Agree	Agree	Strongly Agree	NA

7. Every student here needs a personal computer.					
Strongly Disagree	Disagree	Neither Disagree nor Agree	Agree	Strongly Agree	NA

8. The computer labs on campus are adequate.					
Strongly Disagree	Disagree	Neither Disagree nor Agree	Agree	Strongly Agree	NA

9. The food in the dining hall is good.

Strongly Disagree	Disagree	Neither Disagree nor Agree	Agree	Strongly Agree	NA

10. The food in the dining hall lacks variety.

Strongly Disagree	Disagree	Neither Disagree nor Agree	Agree	Strongly Agree	NA

11. The dorms here are nice.

Strongly Disagree	Disagree	Neither Disagree nor Agree	Agree	Strongly Agree	NA

12. This is a campus that strives for diversity.

Strongly Disagree	Disagree	Neither Disagree nor Agree	Agree	Strongly Agree	NA

13. The student population here is not very diverse.

Strongly Disagree	Disagree	Neither Disagree nor Agree	Agree	Strongly Agree	NA

14. There is a good sports program here.

Strongly Disagree	Disagree	Neither Disagree nor Agree	Agree	Strongly Agree	NA

15. How satisfied are you with your experience as a student?

Very Dissatisfied	Dissatisfied	Neither Dissatisfied Nor Satisfied	Satisfied	Very Satisfied

16. Do you intend to stay and graduate from here?

Yes	No	Not Sure Although no plan to leave	Not Sure Tentative plans to leave

17. How satisfied are you here?

Very Dissatisfied	Dissatisfied	Neither Dissatisfied Nor Satisfied	Satisfied	Very Satisfied

18. I would recommend this university to an incoming freshman.

Strongly Disagree	Disagree	Neither Disagree nor Agree	Agree	Strongly Agree	NA

19. I would recommend this university to a transfer student.

Strongly Disagree	Disagree	Neither Disagree nor Agree	Agree	Strongly Agree	NA

20. What do you think is the best thing about this university?

21. What do you think is the worst thing about this university?

School Survey Activity—Types of Data	*Worksheet*

Qualitative Data: Classified based on characteristics and not measured in amounts.

Quantitative Data: Measured in and indicates amounts (e.g., number present).

Four Traditional Measurement Scales:

- *Nominal Scale*

  Used for identification and classification with no quantitative properties. Each score represents belonging to a group, not an amount. For example, if a class were split into males and females, then this would be a nominal scale.

  The nominal scale can represent qualitative data and is the most basic measurement scale. Membership in one category precludes membership in another group. For ease of understanding, nominal scales often assign numbers to the categories (e.g., Males = 1, Females = 2). However, the number has no inherent value associated with it and is used only for identification, so a female (assigned a 2) is not any better or worse than a male (assigned a 1).

  The **mode** is the preferred measure of central tendency when the data are nominal.

- *Ordinal*

  Scores indicate rank order. Categories are more than merely different and can be ranked in order from highest to lowest or from best to worst. For example, if a class were split according to grade (i.e., A, B, C, D, F), then this would be an ordinal scale.

  There is some disagreement about whether ordinal data represent qualitative or quantitative data. Although ordinal data can be ranked, nothing can be said about data between the ranks. That is to say, it is known that an A is higher than a B, but it can't be known by how much. It is possible the A (i.e., 90%) may only differ from the B (i.e., 89%) by one point. However, it is equally possible that the A (i.e., 99%) differs from the B (i.e., 80%) by 19 points.

  The **median** is the preferred measure of central tendency when the data are ordinal.

- *Interval/Ratio*

  Interval scales have scores that represent an actual quantity with an equal amount of separation/spacing between the scores. Interval scores do not contain a true zero. For example, if a class were organized based on IQ score, this would be an interval scale. There is not a true zero here because one cannot score a zero (indicating a complete lack of intelligence) on the IQ test, and we cannot say that someone who scores a 100 is twice as smart as someone who scored a 50.

Ratio scales, on the other hand, also have scores that represent an actual quantity with an equal amount of separation/spacing between the scores. However, ratio scales contain a true zero. For example, if a class were organized based on the time it took to complete the first exam, this would be a ratio scale. There is a true zero here because it is possible to take no time to complete the exam (e.g., the student did not attempt the exam at all), and if a student takes an hour, then this is twice as long as a student who takes 30 minutes to complete the exam.

The appropriate way to present data and the statistical tests are identical for interval and ratio scales.

The **mean** is the preferred measure of central tendency when the data are interval/ratio *and* normally distributed. If the data are **skewed,** then the median is the preferred measure of central tendency.

GENERAL TYPES OF DATA QUESTIONS

1. There is a controversy among social science researchers regarding multiple-choice measures, such as Likert-type questions (e.g., 1 = Strongly Disagree, 2 = Disagree, 3 = Neither Agree nor Disagree, 4 = Agree, 5 = Strongly Agree). Some researchers consider these types of questions to be ordinal and some consider them to be interval. Which do you consider them to be, ordinal or interval? Why?

   a. What are the possible ramifications of classifying the questions as ordinal?

   b. What are the possible ramifications of classifying the questions as interval?

2. Do you think ordinal data are better classified as quantitative or qualitative? Why?

3. When is the median the best measure of central tendency to report?

4. In social science research, which do you think you will encounter more, nominal, ordinal, or interval/ratio scales? Why?

SCHOOL SURVEY TYPES OF DATA QUESTIONS

1. Identify a question on the survey that is nominal.

    a. What measure of central tendency should be used to report the data from this question?

2. Identify a question on the survey that is ordinal.

    a. What measure of central tendency should be used to report the data from this question?

3. Are any of the questions on the survey ratio? If so, what are they?

4. Identify a question on the survey that is interval/ratio *and* likely has skewed data.

5. In addition to the nominal questions, there are also qualitative questions in the form of the open-ended questions at the end. How do you think the data collected from these questions are different than the data collected from the other questions?

   a. Which type of data would you prefer to work with, qualitative or quantitative? Why?

School Survey Activity—Sampling	*Worksheet*

Population: Contains the entire set of the individuals or objects of interest.

Sample: Is ALWAYS a selected subset of the population.

Population and sample are not static terms! A group that represents a population in one situation (e.g., students at your university) may represent a sample (e.g., selected from students at all universities) in another situation.

There are two main types of sampling, *probability* and *nonprobability* sampling, with one key difference between them. Probability sampling involves random selection, while nonprobability sampling does not. When each unit (individual or group) has an equal chance of being selected for the population, this is random selection.

Probability Sampling: There is a specific (and known) probability of being selected for the sample associated with each person in the population. There is randomness in the selection process.

- *Simple Random Sampling*

  Every person in the population has an equal chance of being selected for the sample.

  For example, if the names of every single student at your university were placed into a hat and then Susan B. Researcher closes her eyes and pulls out 80 names, this is simple random sampling.

  Simple random sampling is simple and effective. However, it is not always possible to conduct simple random sampling.

- *Stratified Random Sampling*

  The population is stratified (i.e., classified into subgroups) by the researcher, and the sample is chosen by randomly selecting people from each stratum. For example, if the undergraduate population was first split by the researcher into classes (e.g., freshmen, sophomores, juniors, and seniors) and Susan B. Researcher then randomly selects students from each class, this is stratified random sampling.

  There are two types of stratified random sampling, proportionate (the percentage selected from each stratum is equal) and disproportionate (the percentage selected from each stratum is unequal). In general, stratified random sampling ensures that the sample will reflect the composition of the population on the stratified dimension. However, there are numerous ways to stratify the sample.

- *Cluster Sampling*

  Existing "clusters" of people within the population are identified, and the entire cluster is sampled. Once a cluster is identified, all of the people in the cluster are included in the sample. For example, if Susan B. Researcher was provided with a list of all of the classes at your university, these would be the clusters. If she then randomly selects four classes and includes all of the members of each of those classes in her study, this is cluster sampling.

Cluster sampling is most often employed to reach large geographic areas without having to travel all over the country (or world). It is often a multistage process where large clusters (e.g., states) are selected and then smaller clusters (e.g., companies) are selected. For phone or mail surveys, cluster sampling is often unnecessary because a broad audience can be easily (and inexpensively) reached.

Nonprobability Sampling: There is not a specific (or known) probability of being selected for the sample associated with each person in the population. This selection process is not random (i.e., not every person in the population has an equal chance of being selected).

- *Convenience Sampling*

Participants are selected because of their availability. Participants are selected because, quite simply, they are there. For example, if Susan B. Researcher selects the first 20 people to arrive in the cafeteria for breakfast who were willing to participate, this is convenience sampling.

This type of sampling is also frequently called accidental, or haphazard, sampling because you "happen across" a sample. Although convenient, this method of sampling may not be an accurate reflection of the population.

- *Purposive Sampling*

Participants are selected for the purpose of ensuring the sample is of a similar composition as the population. For example, Susan B. Researcher knows that 52% of the university population is female, so she intentionally solicits 52 females and 48 males for inclusion in the sample.

As with stratified random sampling, purposive sampling ensures that the sample will reflect the composition of the population on the selected dimension. However, since the sample is not random it is not possible to know how well the sample represents the population.

GENERAL SAMPLING QUESTIONS

1. Why is simple random sampling not always possible? What are some barriers to conducting this type of sampling?

2. With stratified random sampling, how does the researcher select the appropriate stratification dimension?

3. Was cluster sampling necessary in the Susan B. Researcher example above?

4. In the convenience sampling example above, Susan B. Researcher selected people who went to the cafeteria for breakfast. Do you eat breakfast in the cafeteria every morning?

   a. How might you be different from someone who arrives at the cafeteria at 8 a.m. every morning?

   b. How might you be similar to someone who arrives at the cafeteria at 8 a.m. every morning?

   c. How might these two factors influence the results?

5. For purposive sampling, how might a person who agrees to participate in a study be different from a person who does not agree to participate in a study?

   a. How might this influence the results?

SCHOOL SURVEY SAMPLING QUESTIONS

1. The school survey data you collected represent a sample. What is the population from which it was drawn?

2. Do you think this sample adequately represents the population? Why or why not?

3. What method of sampling was used for this survey?

    a. Why do you think this method was selected?

    b. What would have been the ideal method to use?

    c. Why do you think this method was not used?

School Survey Activity—Validity	*Worksheet*

Validity examines the accuracy of a measure. To do that, validity addresses two main questions: What is being measured? And to what extent is that which is being measured similar to what was supposed to be measured? A related issue is reliability. Reliability refers to the consistency of a measure. Reliability is a necessary but insufficient condition of validity. A measure that returns inconsistent results will never be valid.

Types of Validity

- *Face Validity*

  This is the simplest measure of validity. A measure has high face validity if it appears to measure what it purports to be measuring. On its face, does it look as if it measures what it is designed to measure?

  Face validity is not a technical measure of validity and is typically assessed by the people taking and/or administering the measure, not a trained professional. Face validity is not enough to conclude a measure is valid.

- *Content Validity*

  This assesses how comprehensive a measure is with regards to the amount of content covered from the construct in question. For example, for an intelligence test to have content validity, it must cover all of the areas of intelligence. An intelligence test that includes only reading comprehension would have low content validity.

  Content validity is an important but difficult concept to obtain. The best way to determine if there is content validity is to have an expert examine the measure.

- *Construct Validity*

  This measure assesses how valid a selected measure is at measuring what it is intended to measure (i.e., the theoretical construct). To put it another way, a valid measure assesses the construct we intend to study. If, for example, we want to study intelligence, a measure with high construct validity will accurately and parsimoniously measure intelligence. A measure lacking in construct validity will fail to measure intelligence or will measure something in addition to intelligence (e.g., culture specific trivia).

  If a measure is high in construct validity, it is expected to be related to similar measures. So John Q. Undergraduate's score on an intelligence test is expected to be related (although not identical) to his American College Testing (ACT) score. This is called *convergent* validity. Likewise, it is expected that measure will not be related to measures that are unrelated to intelligence. So John Q. Undergraduate's score on the intelligence test is not expected to be related to his blood type. This is called *divergent/discriminant* validity.

In addition to convergent/divergent validity, if a measure is high in construct validity, it is expected that there will be *predictive and concurrent* validity. If there is predictive validity, then performance on the measure in question can be used to predict performance on a similar measure to be completed in the future. In other words, using John Q. Undergraduate's intelligence score, it should be possible to predict his future performance on the Graduate Record Examinations (GRE) test.

If there is concurrent validity, then performance on the measure in question can be used to predict performance on a similar measure that is completed at the same time. If John Q. Undergraduate completes an abbreviated version of an intelligence test and the complete version of the intelligence test in the same testing period, then the abbreviated version should accurately predict his score on the complete version.

GENERAL VALIDITY QUESTIONS

1. What type of validity do you think is the most important? Why?

2. What type of validity do you think is the least important? Why?

3. Describe the difference between convergent and divergent validity.

4. Describe the difference between predictive and concurrent validity.

SCHOOL SURVEY TYPES OF DATA QUESTIONS

1. The survey is designed to collect undergraduates' perceptions of their university. Do you think the survey has face validity? Why or why not?

2. As a current undergraduate student, you can be considered the expert on the undergraduate experience. With that in mind, do you think the survey has content validity?

   a. What, if anything, do you think is missing?

3. What would be an item (not included on the survey) that could be used to assess convergent validity?

4. What would be an item (not included on the survey) that could be used to assess divergent/ discriminant validity?

5. There is a question on the survey that is designed to get at the idea of predictive validity. Which question is it?

   a. Do you think it accurately assesses predictive validity? Why or why not?

6. There is a question on the survey that is designed to get at the idea of concurrent validity. Which question is it?

   a. Do you think it accurately assesses concurrent validity? Why or why not?

Dr. Stan Nussbaum

GMI Research Services and Wheaton College

OVERVIEW

Designing field questions is of utmost importance to the research process, and it demands precision and finesse, yet the skill need not be a chore to acquire. The Teacup Olympics will help get you through this important step in your project, enabling you to spot and improve a mediocre question even if you wrote it yourself. You may be pleasantly surprised at the high quality questions you can produce as you begin to grasp and apply the six basics of Teacup question design.

INSTRUCTIONS

Prior to the game, you need to have chosen your research topic, articulated your central research question, and listed one to four hypotheses related to it. Fill that information into the top part of Worksheet 1 so you can easily refer to it during the Olympic game. Do not write your three field questions yet.

When you have filled in the above information, the instructor will explain the six basic criteria for field research questions.[1] They are the "Teacup" criteria that will be judged during this Olympic competition:

1. Tolerable (not too threatening)

Bad example. About how often do you exaggerate the amounts on your expense reports: (a) usually or always, (b) sometimes, (c) rarely, (d) seldom or never.

Good adjustment or alternative. How often do you think people in this company exaggerate the amounts on their expense reports: (a) usually or always, (b) sometimes, (c) rarely, (d) seldom or never.

2. Essential (for testing one or more of the hypotheses)

Note: The examples below work only if you know that the central research question was, "What does the staff of the Uganda Revenue Authority believe are the appropriate incentives that can motivate the building of a culture of integrity in the department?" One of the hypotheses was that an open system of promotions would be a strong incentive.

---

[1] Your instructor may alter the number and/or names of the criteria so the game flexes to fit the normal content and emphasis of the course.

Bad example. Agree or disagree: The integrity of the department is worse than it was 5 years ago because the country's economy is worse in general. (Scale from strongly agree to strongly disagree.)

Good adjustment or alternative. A more open system of staff promotions would be a strong incentive for staff to work with integrity. (Scale from strongly agree to strongly disagree.)

3. Answerable (within the knowledge and thought pattern of the respondent)

Bad example (posed to a fourth grader). "What are the most useful improvements your teacher has made during this school year?"

Good adjustment or alternative. "What does your teacher do to make boring subjects more interesting for the class?"

4. Clear (to the respondent not just the researcher)

Bad example. How much would our effectiveness go up if we had more training? (a) a lot, (b) somewhat, (c) a little.

Good adjustment or alternative. How much would our effectiveness go up if we had more on-the-job training provided during our regular working hours? (a) a lot, (b) somewhat, (c) a little.

5. Unbiased (leaving all options open for the respondent)

Bad example. Is your marriage difficult these days, or is it worse than that?

Good adjustment or alternative. On a scale of 1 to 10 with 10 being most positive, how are you and your wife getting along? (Note that in some circumstances, this question might still violate the "Tolerable" criterion.)

6. Penetrating (revealing what the researcher really wants to discover).

Bad example. Why didn't the project work out as planned?

Good adjustment or alternative. Would you say that the project's failure was mostly due to inadequate staffing? Why or why not?

After discussing the criteria, try to write three questions that meet all six of them (bottom of Worksheet 1). Your questions must relate to at least one of your hypotheses. After writing, check each question against the Teacup criteria and make any improvements you can. Then, choose the best of your three questions since you will be allowed to use only one question if you are chosen as a contestant. (Short questions work better than long ones for the game, so try to choose a shortish question even if it is not absolutely your best one.)

Now, you are ready. Let the games begin! You will participate continuously in the game, taking the role of contestant, judge, or spectator at any given time as assigned by the instructor. Spectators are just as involved as contestants and judges, perhaps even more so, though they are under less pressure because they can hide their mistakes.

To begin play, the instructor will choose the first contestant and a panel of six judges. Seated before the panel, the contestant reads his or her topic and research question from the top of Worksheet 1, then, the best of his or her questions and the hypothesis which the question relates to. *The contestant may not add any explanation at all* at this stage of the game. The judges base their judgment entirely on the words read from the worksheet. Judges may ask the contestant to reread the question and/or other information, but they make no comment before they reveal their scores.

Each judge scores the question on only one of the six criteria (one judge for each criterion). This is slightly tricky because it is different than judging during the real Olympics, where each judge is judging the performance as a whole. For example, in this game, the judge who is judging "Tolerability" may notice that a question is weak because it is unclear, but that should not in any way affect the score he or she gives it. A different judge will score it for "Clarity." One judge, one criterion.

This is crucial to the value of the game as a learning game rather than a competition. Comparing the total score of one contestant with another or dividing the contestants into teams and keeping score that way is unhelpful in this game because it does not tell any contestant how or where to improve. Contestants need individual scores on individual criteria.

While the judges are scoring, the spectators also score the question, but each spectator scores the question on all six criteria instead of just one like the judges do. A scorecard will be provided to the spectators, so they can score each question for themselves before the judges reveal their scores. This allows spectators to practice using all the criteria at once, which is the skill they will need later when they develop their full questionnaires.

The instructor will call for the judges to hold up their scores all at once, using the number cards provided. These should be kept in view during the discussion. The instructor is the moderator (or referee if things start to go badly). As a general guideline, judges will comment first, then spectators (who may ask judges to explain their scores and/or suggest alternate scores), and finally the contestant. It is not necessary for every judge to comment on every question.

Under criticism from judges and/or spectators, contestants naturally want to justify themselves by explaining the intentions behind their question: "What I meant was. . ." That phrase is not allowed in the game because it is not allowed during actual field research. Researchers will bias the respondents and spoil the data if they start explaining the questions to them. The written question standing alone must say exactly what the researcher means.

Therefore, contestants should consciously put out of their minds the default thought, Why can't these people understand my perfectly good question? Instead they should ask themselves, How could I alter this question so that fewer people would miss my point and more would give me the information I am looking for? Then the game can help them. (Do not set your sights on idiot-proof questions, however. As someone has observed, "It is impossible to make a question idiot-proof because idiots are so clever.")

After each contestant is finished, the instructor will call the next one. He or she may change or rearrange the judges from time to time during the game. If time allows after the game, then you may revise your three questions and test your revisions with one or two other participants.

This is a learning game that is equipping you to write high quality questions that will contribute to a good grade via your fieldwork and research report. The Teacup criteria are not all you need to know about question writing, but they cover many of the fundamentals, and they give you a manageable point of reference for self-checking your questions before you field-test.

The Teacup Olympics—Teacup Contestants	Worksheet

Your topic (10 words or less)

State your central research question about this topic

Provide one to four hypotheses (possible answers to this question)

List three field questions that meet Teacup criteria:

(*Note*: Each question should elicit responses that will help you prove, disprove, or modify at least one of your hypotheses.)

1.

2.

3.

The Teacup Olympics—Teacup Spectator's Scorecard	Worksheet

Score each contestant's question on all six criteria. Enter your scores in the table before the judges reveal theirs. Then, compare your scores to their scores. The more comfortable you get with analyzing questions by these criteria during the game, the easier it will be for you later to design your full questionnaires.

Scoring: 4 = excellent, 3 = good, 2 = acceptable, 1 = poor, 0 = disqualified

Contestant's name	Tolerable	Essential	Answerable	Clear	Unbiased	Penetrating

THE SIX BASIC CRITERIA

Tolerable (not too threatening)

Essential (for testing one or more of the hypotheses)

Answerable (within the knowledge and thought pattern of the respondent)

Clear (to the respondent not just the researcher)

Unbiased (leaving all options open for the respondent)

Penetrating (revealing what the researcher really wants to discover)

CHAPTER 4

QUALITATIVE METHODS, OBSERVATIONAL METHODS

I n research methods, there are two main types of data, qualitative and quantitative, each with its own particular benefits. This chapter is about the gathering and analyzing of qualitative data through observational methods. This book contains two methods of gathering qualitative data, observational and interview. Interview methods will be covered in the next chapter.

Qualitative data are data that are gathered through open-ended questions, interviews, observations, content analysis, focus groups, and so forth. If a survey question is not multiple choice, then the answer is generally considered qualitative datum. The question, what are some of your hobbies? is open-ended; that means that you could literally say any activity is a hobby, and it would fit in. If it were quantitative (or closed-ended), then the answers would be multiple choice and assigned a numerical value, as for instance, in the question, Which hobby most closely matches your interests, A, B, C, et cetera?

The major practical difference between the two types of data is that quantitative data lend themselves to quantitative analysis. Since most quantitative data are multiple choice, people are naturally broken down into predetermined categories and very easy to compare with each other. Qualitative data require more effort to break them into categories, and the categories have to be created after the data have been gathered. We call the process of analyzing and breaking qualitative data into categories coding and cleaning, and it requires imagination.

This chapter focuses on the qualitative data that are gathered through observational methods—perhaps the most unobtrusive way of gathering data. You will learn to look at spaces in a new way, as though you had never seen them, take note of things that normally you take for granted. You will learn to quantify phenomena and see that by doing this, you can draw new and exciting conclusions about the mundane places and events that surround us.

EXPLORING THE MUNDANE: AN EXERCISE USING ETHNOMETHODOLOGICAL RESEARCH METHODS TO EXAMINE EVERYDAY SPACES

Judith E. Rosenstein

United States Naval Academy

INSTRUCTIONS

In your groups, go out and explore the _____. What do you learn from the _____? As a group, ask yourselves what it is that you want to know. Then, consider how best to get that information. In other words, what research methods are going to best provide you with the answers to your questions (e.g., observation, talking with people using the _____, etc.)? How you go about doing this is up to you. Report back in 20 minutes.

GRADING

Your grade will be based on the instructor's assessment of your participation in the activity.

Exploring the Mundane: An Exercise Using Ethnomethodological Research Methods to Examine Everyday Spaces	*Worksheet*

INSTRUCTIONS

In one to two pages, reflect back on your experience exploring the _____.
Here are some questions to consider as you write your paper:

1. How did your choice of research methods help or hinder your quest to learn about the space?

2. How does your current view of _____ compare with your earlier view of it?

3. How easy or difficult was it to look at a familiar place as though you had never been there before?

4. How, if at all, will this experience influence how you look at the world?

FINDING THE FIELD

Sandy Sulzer

University of Wisconsin, Madison

OVERVIEW

This is your first attempt at using methods, and rather than telling you how to do a field observation, you will attempt it with very little direction, learn from it, and come together as a class to develop guidelines for future researchers who want to know how to tackle their first field observation.

INSTRUCTIONS

Your instructions for this exercise are simple—go do a field observation. Refer to the fieldnotes guidelines for detailed instructions.

You will turn in your fieldnotes as well as a two- to four-page paper outlining how you did your research, what makes it good or strong, and what you would improve if you did it again.

GRADING

Your grade will be based on the instructor's assessment of your participation in the activity using the following criteria:

1. STRUCTURE: Begin your paper with a brief description of your fieldwork, which is a concise yet comprehensive statement of your project. Each paragraph should have a topic sentence and three to five sentences that clearly support that topic sentence. Each paragraph should explain *one* idea, not three or four, and each paragraph should have a clear connection to the next (i.e., pay attention to transitions). End with a strong conclusion about implications for future research.

2. EVIDENCE: Each paragraph should advance your argument that you did good science, if you think you achieved that. When possible, support your methods choices with evidence from academic sources, always remembering to explain what your evidence means and offering specific insights. Include ample discussion of what you would do differently next time.

3. STYLE: Clarity comes from knowing what you mean and saying it plainly. Do not try to write like a writer; write like a person who wants to be understood. Write with active verbs, not the passive voice (e.g., do not start sentences with "It is" or "There are"). Revise your paper to remove wordiness, redundancy, passive voice, and run-on sentences. Also, make sure that your grammar and spelling are correct. Careless errors will lower your grade.

4. ORIGINALITY: Although you can get a good grade (B) for a paper based on arguments presented in lectures or course readings, excellent papers (A) must offer more original insights and arguments. Build on evidence and arguments from the course, but push your insights further.

Finding the Field	*Fieldnotes Guidelines*

For this assignment, you will be turning in a two- to four-page, double-spaced justification of how you did your research: What makes it good or strong, and what you would improve if you did it again.

You won't be told how to do each step of the process, but here are some guidelines and things to think of before you get started.

1. Where will you observe?

There are many locations we pass through in our day-to-day lives and others we typically don't spend time in, due to habit, differing cultures or differing interests. Will you choose somewhere familiar or unfamiliar? How does this change how you approach observing? Will you stand out or blend in? Will standing out or fitting in change what you can observe? Perhaps if you are white and observe in a community center in a black neighborhood, then you will stand out as an outsider. As the researcher, you will be making choices about the location, and as a class, we will discuss how what we've found differed depending on the location chosen.

It is also important to think about the ethics of where one observes. For this assignment, observations should be done only in a clearly public space. *Public* here means a space in which someone has a reasonable expectation of being observed. Locker rooms, bathrooms, and inside someone's home are not public spaces. If you're in doubt, always ask permission or choose a different location. It's important to be in a public area so that you aren't violating someone's privacy or the anonymity people can maintain in public. For example, observing student–professor conversations in a professor's office could reveal other students grades and information they didn't intend for their peers to know. This would be ethically problematic.

2. What will you observe?

The parameters of this are up to you. Some projects start with a research question, many do not. Do you have something you'd like to figure out or learn more about? Oftentimes, having a personal interest in your research makes it more fun to do. While observing at the library to collect data on study habits is convenient, it may not be very interesting to you. Instead, you might use this opportunity to record data on something you find engaging. As the researchers, you get to make a decision about what you think is important and then collect data that fit those priorities. After each group finishes their observations, we will have a conversation about what each group decided to look at and how this affected their findings and research process.

3. When will you observe?

Sometimes, this question matters more than others. For example, if you wanted to observe people going into movie theaters, you'd observe vastly different amounts of people entering on a Friday night versus a Tuesday morning. Depending on what you hope to learn, you might want to observe at both of these times to get a sense of the range of people. Or you might want to focus in on just the weekends or just matinees. When you observe is a decision that revolves around what you are trying to see. Then, you make an educated guess about how your observations might vary by time of day, or day of week, and make decisions accordingly about the best times to watch. Or if you're completely uncertain, you may decide that you'll have to observe at multiple times because you don't have a good sense of what kind of variation there is.

4. How will you record your observations?

Different researchers develop different ways to write down what they see. But one thing most agree on is that if you don't record anything, it can be hard to remember everything, and this hurts the quality of your data. Some go so far as to say that if something isn't written down, then it is not datum: If it's not in your notes, it didn't happen. Other times, it's not possible to record everything at the time, and some scholars end up writing up more detailed notes in private after finishing their observations. However you decide to record your notes, *if* you decide to do so, plan on bringing a copy with you to show your classmates. This way we can learn from each other and discover many different approaches to note taking, and evaluate what kinds work best in what situations.

5. What should you write up?

The grading criteria are below, but an important thing to think about in addition to the grading criteria is the idea of self-reflexivity. It is important in this assignment, and in all research, to be reflective and conscious of the choices you made as well as what the possible ramifications of those choices are. If you are a man observing in a mostly female space, then how do you think that affected what you observed? Were things different because you were present? Did you do anything to fit in better? Did you tell people why you were there, or remain silent? How do you think the choice to tell people you were a researcher, or not, affected what you observed? Do you think your identity was completely irrelevant to what you saw, and if so, why?

Research is always done by real people. There is no way to complete a research project from beginning to end without human agency. So it is good to think about how each of us as individuals puts her or his stamp on that process or perhaps tried to avoid putting a stamp on the process. For this reason, I encourage you to be as open as possible about what you think went well or what could have gone better. You will not be evaluated on presenting a picture of the perfect research project but rather graded on your ability to see how choices you made led to better or worse results. *Good* science is a concept open for debate. Each scholar gets to decide on some level what kind of ideal they are shooting for and to design their projects accordingly.

6. What if you get stuck?

It's OK to come in and ask questions if you get stuck, but I won't answer questions about *how* to do the project. You are the researcher in charge here, and your decisions are the ones you will have to defend. The point isn't to do someone else's version of a good project—but your own. Being able to articulate what choices you made and why is a big part of doing research and an important part of every project and write-up. If you did a project a certain way because I told you to, you might not have a chance to figure out for yourself the reasoning behind each choice in the process. That reasoning is the basis of what makes for a good researcher, so think of that when you get to a point where you're not sure what to do next. There are no wrong choices, just opportunities to learn.

Finding the Field	*Handout*

General Notes

The point is not for you to complete the assignment in a regimented way but for you to demonstrate your own perspective on what good field research looks like, as well as your experience confronting the reality of actually doing the research rather than simply talking about how one "should" do a field observation.

General Dos and Don'ts

Selecting a location for a field observation can be tricky, so before you decide where to begin your research, ask yourself a few questions about the place you've chosen.

1. Is it safe for me to be here? Am I in the way of any oncoming vehicles? Is it well lit and somewhere I feel comfortable?

2. Is it respectful for me to be here? Am I intruding on anyone's sacred space? Am I disrupting anything? Am I making the people I'm observing visibly uncomfortable?

And because originality is a part of your grade, you might want to consider somewhere other than the library or student union. However, please be mindful of the "General Dos and Don'ts" list above!

Your Final Paper

You will be graded on how well you make a case for having done good science, including acknowledging what you could have done better in two to four pages. The "what you could have done better" part is your opportunity to showcase what you learned from the activity, and it should take center stage. Your summary of your field observation itself should be brief. Feel free to reference our course readings or outside research in making your case about why you chose the methods you chose.

Working as a Team

If you have any problems in your partnership, please contact your instructor, and consider turning in separate research justifications if that would resolve concerns about uneven participation. It is unethical and ill-advised to turn in a pair assignment in which one person did 70% or more of the work.

Finding the Field	**Worksheet**

Use this space to take notes as we go around the class and talk about our experiences in the field. By documenting the details of each group's process, we can then discuss how to do field research using our collective wisdom. After everyone has shared, we will then create a step-by-step list of how to do field research that we'd give a friend if it was their first time going into the field.

Group Members	Research Site	Times/Days of Observation	What Was Observed	Major Successes	Major Difficulties
1. 2.					
1. 2.					
1. 2.					
1. 2.					
1. 2.					
1. 2.					

DO YOU SEE WHAT I SEE? OBSERVATIONAL METHODS ON CAMPUS

Venezia Michalsen, PhD

Montclair State University

OVERVIEW

Observational research methods can be a powerful way to examine social phenomena and are particularly useful as a tool to complement findings from other methods. However, observational methods are quite prone to problems with reliability and validity. In this exercise, you and your classmates will be conducting an observation and comparing your results. After completing this exercise, you should have new insight into the importance of clear **operationalization** of variables, unobtrusive measures, triangulation with other methods, and comparison of ratings between observers.

INSTRUCTIONS

There are many ways to measure social phenomena, such as levels of school spirit at a particular university. For example, a researcher might conduct a telephone survey to ask randomly selected students how much school spirit they have on a scale of one to five. Another researcher might use archival data to measure attendance at school events over time. A third researcher might decide to use a *direct observation* method to measure school spirit. Direct observations have a number of benefits over other methods. For example, observations avoid problems with respondents' poor memory and self-serving distortions often found using survey methods. However, observation methods have problems of their own: Observers bring their own set of preconceptions to what they see, and they may not see everything during an observation. Finally, the mere presence of an observer may change the behavior of those being observed, affecting the results of the study.

Your class will be going, as a group, to a public place where there are people to observe. Your instructor will designate a space for you to conduct your observation of the people who are in that space. You will be assigned a variable to observe by your instructor. On the worksheet provided, count the number of times you observe your assigned phenomenon within the designated time frame. After the observation is completed, you will compare your results to those of your classmates, and discuss the implications of your results.

GRADING

This assignment will be graded solely on the basis of your participation in the activity and discussion.

Do You See What I See? *Observational Methods on Campus*	*Worksheet*

Observation details

Start time: _____   End time: _____

Borders of observation space: _____

Variable details

Variable to observe (assigned by instructor): _____

How will you operationalize this variable? That is, how will you know your variable when you see it? _____

_____

Example for the variable *school spirit*: a person wearing clothing with the school logo on it will be counted as having "school spirit."

Make a mark every time you observe your variable:

SOUTH PARK ANALYSIS

Kristin L. Cherry, PhD

Central Methodist University

INSTRUCTIONS

For this assignment, you will be performing a content analysis of the popular TV show *South Park*. Your instructor will assign you a number between 1 and 5. Then, refer to the list below to determine what particular social behavior you will be watching for and counting in this episode. Please work individually. Please list and count each time you see the behavior in this episode of *South Park*.

Social behaviors to watch for are the following:

1. Please list any time that you hear the characters refer to political issues, parties, or references to politics.

2. Please list any male stereotype that is portrayed in this episode. List things that tell us how males "should" act. Include messages that tell young boys what behavior is cool and acceptable.

3. Please list every animal and human that is killed during the episode, with a tally mark for how many of each is killed.

4. List any foul language that you hear. Please list the phrase, and if you hear it more than once, then make a tally mark for each instance.

5. Please list any crude behavior that is displayed or talked about. This includes, but is not limited to, burping, vomiting, farting, urination, or defecation.

INSTRUCTIONS—STEP 1 (CONTENT ANALYSIS)

First, you will break up into a group with individuals with corresponding numbers. Compare and discuss your findings with your group.

Present your group's findings to the class and discuss your results.

After the discussion, your group will develop a common code sheet that could be used to help researchers in a future content analysis.

INSTRUCTIONS—STEP 2 (QUESTIONNAIRE DESIGN)

Return to the same group you worked with in Step 1. Review your findings from the content analysis.

Your next assignment is to construct a questionnaire to examine audience perceptions of *South Park*. Your group should come up with 10 to 15 questions that could provide researchers with more information about how audiences perceive the TV show *South Park*, focusing on your group's specific observed behavior.

After your group has finished your survey, give your survey to another group to pretest. When pretesting another group's survey, assess the survey based on the student critique worksheet.

After the survey has been pretested, return it to the original group. When you receive your pretested survey, you may make any changes before turning in your completed survey for grading.

GRADING

Your instructor will provide grading instructions for this exercise.

South Park Analysis	**Student Critique Worksheet**

This Worksheet is designed to assess the quality of your survey

1. Examine the questions on your survey.

    a. Is the language appropriate?

    b. Are questions in full sentences?

    c. Did you avoid double-barreled questions?

    d. Did you avoid jargon and slang?

    e. Did you avoid abbreviations?

    f. Did you avoid negative questions?

    g. Did you avoid leading, or loaded, questions?

    h. Did you avoid emotional language?

    i. Did you avoid **prestige bias**?

    j. Did you avoid false premises?

    k. Did you avoid double negatives?

2. Examine your categories for question responses.

    a. Are your categories **mutually exclusive**?

    b. Do your categories exhaust all possible answers?

    c. Are the categories balanced?

3. Examine the overall survey.

    a. Did you find any language or vocabulary that was unclear or abstract?

    b. Were all the questions interpreted the same by everyone in the pretest group?

    c. Can all of the questions be answered with the responses given?

    d. When pretesting, did the respondents read and answer each question?

    e. Are all of the questions within the respondents' capabilities?

CHAPTER **5**

QUALITATIVE METHODS, INTERVIEW/FOCUS GROUPS

As discussed in the intro to the last chapter, qualitative data are less structured data that require coding and cleaning to be quantified. One of the most well-known tools of the social science researcher is the *focus group*, and this chapter details how to conduct one, as well as how to guide a one-on-one interview through a technique called **active listening**.

A focus group can be an invaluable method of gathering information, but it has to be properly managed. Without a competent facilitator, the group dynamic can be taken over by an overly aggressive member or by an unusually quiet group. The idea of a focus group is to get people to think about topics they haven't thought about much before. It won't be very useful to hold a focus group on abortion, because most people would walk in with their own views that they have practice defending, which only results in deadlock. However, a focus group on something less controversial, for instance, favorite air freshener scents and why, will cause people to examine their subconscious biases and understand a little more about something they never really thought about. Favorite air freshener scent might be seen as an exceedingly trite discussion topic, but the point is to avoid touching on hot button issues. This chapter offers practice running a focus group, as well as participating in one and designing one from start to finish.

One-on-one interviewing is a different skill from a focus group, and this chapter offers practice in that as well. A Focus Group requires several key skills, including knowing how to follow a conversation without interjecting your own opinions. Another skill is to learn how to guide the conversation without being so rigid that members are not able to speak freely, but by also not letting them speak so freely that the conversation runs off willy nilly. These skills are going to make all the difference in getting the desired results.

Understanding the ethical issues involved with interviewing subjects is crucial, and this chapter touches on that. Getting the right permissions and staying on an ethical track during interviews is very important, for both the reputation of the social sciences and the comfort of the subject.

Finally, just as important as knowing how to conduct a focus group or interview is knowing how to record and analyze the data, and this chapter goes into that as well. Important points include writing down your thoughts immediately after the interview, having someone else on hand to put up points on a whiteboard, recording the conversation, and so on.

Focus groups and interviews are some of the most fun and active elements of social science research, so don't be nervous in approaching them but just have fun!

RESEARCH PROJECT ON QUALITATIVE DATA CODING AND ANALYSIS—CHRISTMAS WISHES

Chunyan Song, PhD

California State University, Chico

OVERVIEW

For this exercise, you will use qualitative data to analyze Christmas Wishes.

INSTRUCTIONS

To successfully complete this assignment, you need to refer to class lectures and to your text-book chapter on qualitative data analysis. You need to work with one or two students in the class on this assignment using the attached worksheets.

If Santa Claus could grant one wish of yours, what would you want it to be? Please submit your answer to the above question together with your age and gender information on the online discussion board before the deadline. After everyone has submitted his or her wishes, please go through the responses in groups and see if you can locate any patterns by age or gender. This will allow you to categorize the data.

1. During conceptualization and open coding, work with your partner(s) to identify and define any emerging concepts. In the process of open coding, you have to revise the concepts or categories probably many times until you get a good set of categories. Please pay special attention to both the extremely large and small categories. You might be able to break down large categories into two or more categories. When you have too many categories with only one or two cases, it does not help to identify patterns later, so you may have to combine some of these smaller categories in a logical way. Note: Categories need to be both exhaustive and mutually exclusive. This means that every response should fit into one and only one of the categories. Use the following tables to record all the categories and the codes you used.

Research Project on Qualitative Data Coding and Analysis—Christmas Wishes	Worksheet

Category/Concept	Definition of Concept	Number of Responses in Category	Percentage of Total	Number Responses Using Identical Words
#1 xxx				For example, 4 used "keyword xxx" and 2 used "keyword xxx"
#2 xxx				
#3 xxx				
#4 xxx				
#5 xxx				
#6 xxx, etc.				
Total				

2. Now, sort the responses by gender and record them on the table below. Any patterns or differences? What causal factors do you think could help to explain the patterns (if any)?

Category/Concept	% Female in Category	% Male in Category	Total Number of Responses in Category
#1 xxx			
#2 xxx			
#3 xxx			
#4 xxx			
#5 xxx			
#6 xxx, etc.			
Total			

3. Now, sort the responses into the following age groups: young (23 or under), older (24–29), oldest (30 or above). Any patterns or differences? What causal factors do you think could help to explain the patterns (if any)? Record the responses using the table below:

Category/Concept	% Young in Category	% Older in Category	% Oldest in Category	Total Number of Responses in Category
#1 xxx				
#2 xxx				
#3 xxx				
#4 xxx				
#5 xxx				
#6 xxx, etc.				
Total				

EXPLORING ETHNOGRAPHY: UNDERSTANDING SPORT COMMUNITIES

Diana Tracy Cohen, PhD

Central Connecticut State University

OVERVIEW

This research project will introduce you to the exciting world of ethnography. Ethnography seeks to gain a detailed understanding about a specific population. For this project, your task is to learn about the details of a specific sport culture. Your sport ethnography will incorporate two methodological approaches, interviewing and observation. Together, these methods will help give you a more comprehensive understanding of people that occupy the specific sport community that you select.

INSTRUCTIONS

Your goal is to gain a deeper understand of the following two issues:

1. Understand the demographics of the sport
   - What types of people participate?
   - How popular is the sport on both a domestic and international level?
   - What different levels of competition are there?

2. Understand the culture of the sport
   - What is the culture of the sport like?
   - Culturally, what makes the sport unique from other sports?
   - What language or artifacts make your sport unique?

This project has four main components:

1. Interviews

You are required to conduct five interviews with people situated within the sport community that you select. Potential respondents could include coaches, varsity athletes, and club athletes. Create an interview guide of approximately 10 questions. These questions should be general in nature. The more specific the question, the more you are limiting the scope of the research. Your instructor will go over an example of an interview guide with you in class. Be prepared to share your interview guide with your peers.

You do not need to be highly rigid in sticking to your interview guide. Instead, see where the conversation takes you. Use your instincts in determining if your participant is straying too far from the topic.

96

As quickly as possible after conducting the interview, write your interview notes. Detail the time, place, and atmosphere of your interview. Write down the key themes discussed by the participant as well as how you felt throughout the course of the interaction. Also, detail any nonverbal communication cues that you observed during the interview.

2. Observation

You are required to observe your sport community two separate times. Each observation should last for approximately 30 minutes. Try your best not to interfere with the activity of the group that you are observing.

During or right after each observation, write a set of observation notes. Detail what you saw. How did the individuals interact with one another? What did you learn about the culture of your sport?

3. Analysis

The final paper requires you to synthesize all of the information that you have learned. The paper should be approximately 10 pages in length, excluding the appendix. Use the final paper checklist as a guide.

4. Presentation

The final step is to present your findings to your peers. Your presentation should be 10 to 15 minutes in length. You are required to use one visual aid in the course of your presentation. Introduce the class to your sport, briefly discuss your methods, and articulate your main findings. A 5-minute question-and-answer period will follow.

GRADING

1. Interview notes (worth 20%)
   * Include five sets of interview notes
   * Be as detailed and thoughtful as possible

2. Observation notes (worth 20%)
   * Include two sets of observation notes
   * Be as detailed and thoughtful as possible

3. Final paper (worth 50%)
   * Address all components listed on the paper checklist
   * Demonstrate a cultural understanding for the sport you selected
   * Be grammatically correct

4. Research presentation (10%)
   * Maintain a loud and clear speaking voice
   * Use a well-constructed visual aid

Final Paper Checklist

Your paper must contain each of the following components.

I. INTRODUCTION

Introduce your **case study**. Frame the community and identify the main questions that you are answering.

- What are your main research questions?
- Has anyone done systematic research on your sport?
- How does your research fit into the larger dialogue about sport and culture?

II. METHODOLOGY

Discuss how you went about conducting your research.

- What are your methods?
- Who did you study? When did you study them?
- Who did you interview? What questions did you ask?
- How did you influence your own study?

III. ANALYSIS

Offer a detailed analysis of your sport. Present your main findings.

- What did you learn about the culture of your sport?
- What did you learn about the demographics of your sport?
- What did you learn in your interviews and observations, respectively?

IV. CONCLUSION

Tell us how your findings contribute to a larger dialogue about sporting culture.

- What are the implications for your findings?
- What future questions are left unanswered?

V. APPENDIX

Attach your interview guide.

OVERVIEW

Focus groups are a common method of collecting qualitative, narrative data for social science research. They are particularly advantageous when researchers seek deep information on topics that participants have not thought a lot about and perhaps do not have strong feelings about. For example, focus groups are popularly used in marketing research, because consumers do not usually spend much time thinking about each item they buy or why they like one item or brand over another. In this example, the discussions on items among a group of consumers can reveal the ranges of reasons for their popularity and the broad strengths and weaknesses of the products.[1] In general, focus groups result in *ranges* and *syntheses* of ideas from the groups' discussions.

One of the main challenges of focus groups, however, is effectively facilitating them to generate useful data. While the groups' discussions constitute the data, discussions can often get sidetracked and group dynamics can result in biased data. For example, one participant with a strong personality might dominate the discussion or lead it down a tangential path. Another reserved participant might contribute very little to the discussion. In such cases, the challenge for the researchers is to manage the dynamics of the discussion to gain broad participation by participants and to truly focus the group on the topics at hand. In these ways, the researchers can ensure the collection of representative and useful data.

This in-class exercise lets you observe and participate in mock focus groups, in order to experience realistic dynamics of the method and to identify useful techniques for facilitating focus groups.

INSTRUCTIONS

There are two focus groups in this exercise. For one, you will participate in the focus group role play, while for the other you will carefully and analytically observe your classmates' role play. The two focus groups and their available roles are summarized in the table below. Your instructor will assign a role to you for each of these role plays, either a character in the role play or an observer of the focus group.

---

[1]On the other hand, focus groups are usually not appropriate for topics that people have strong opinions about, such as abortion or the death penalty. Such topics do not generate a synthesis of ideas or preferences, because individuals' opinions are set and not likely to be swayed. They are also difficult to facilitate because of the debates that can ensue.

If you are assigned a character, you will be given a brief description of your character and a little time to develop details of the character. This is the fun part of the role play, as you consider details of your character's job, family life, income level, and experiences and how all these details affect your character's views on the discussion topic. Be creative here and draw on your inner actor. Find your motivation! The more in-character you are during the role play, the more meaningful the exercise will be.

Focus group topic	Roles

Focus group of nonprofit and government workers on their decisions to enter public service	Characters in the role play (7 to 10):
	• Facilitator (1)
	• Scribe and assistant facilitator (1)
	• Public service employees in the focus group (5 to 8):
	  ○ Executive director of a private nonprofit organization
	  ○ 25-year veteran of law enforcement
	  ○ New teacher in a public school
	  ○ Administrative assistant at the Department of Motor Vehicles
	  ○ Middle manager at a federal agency
	  ○ Postal worker
	  ○ Organizer for an environmental nonprofit organization
	  ○ Immigrant rights worker
	Observers: rest of the class

Focus group of public transportation users on their perceptions of the public transportation system	Characters in the role play (7 to 10): • Facilitator (1) • Scribe and assistant facilitator (1) • Public transportation users in the focus group (5 to 8) ○ Observers: rest of the class

If you are an observer for a role play, use the observer worksheet below to help you critically analyze the dynamics of the focus group. At the end of the role play, the observers will be asked to critique the focus group.

GRADING

This is not a graded assignment. Rather, it is an in-class exercise to spur class discussion on the skills and challenges of facilitating focus groups.

Facilitating Focus Groups and Managing Their Dynamics—Observations	*Worksheet*

As you observe the role play, take notes on the below questions. Try to answer them from the perspective of a researcher, whose overall objective is to get useful data pertaining to the research topic.

Also, remember that you are not judging or grading your classmates. After all, they're acting! Instead, you are analyzing the behaviors exhibited in the focus group and the overall dynamics of the discussion.

1. What is going well in the focus group?

2. What successful tactics do you see in the facilitation of the focus group?

3. What problems, if any, do you see in the focus group?

4. What suggestions do you have on improving the facilitation of the focus group?

EXPLORING THE FOCUS GROUP METHOD: A PRACTICAL EXPERIENCE

Eeva Sointu

Smith College

DESCRIPTION

Focus groups are becoming increasingly significant means of gathering qualitative data from multiple individuals simultaneously. A well-planned focus group offers participants an informal and friendly setting to discuss a shared topic, with the group interaction being the key to the generation of rich and complex data.[2]

This exercise introduces you to the use of focus groups in qualitative research. In groups of 9 to 12 students, you will develop a focus group topic guide as well as other materials needed for a successful focus group. Two members of your group will use the materials that were collectively developed to run your focus group with another group of students. Meanwhile, the rest of your group will act as participants for the facilitators from another group. The class following the focus group will revolve around discussing focus group methodology. You are also invited to use your sociological imaginations to analyze the findings.

LEARNING OBJECTIVES

- To design a focus group
- To develop a topic guide
- To develop prompts to guide focus group discussion
- To gain experience of facilitating a focus group
- To understand the practicalities involved in using focus groups in your research
- To experience a focus group as a participant
- To understand the usefulness of the focus group method for social research
- To understand group dynamics in focus groups
- To understand research ethics in the context of focus group research

---

[2] Breen, Rosanna L. (2006). A practical guide to focus-group research. *Journal of Geography in Higher Education*, *30*(3), 463–475.

Tonkiss, Fran. (2004). Using focus groups. In C. Seale (Ed.), *Researching society and culture* (pp. 193–206). London: Sage.

Onwuegbuzie, Anthony J., Dickinson, Wendy B., Leech, Nancy L., Zoran, & Annmarie G. (2009). A qualitative framework for collecting and analyzing data in focus group research. *International Journal of Qualitative Methods, 8*(3), 1–21.

GRADING CRITERIA

You are graded both individually and in groups. The individual grade forms 20% of the final grade for the exercise, while the grade for your group forms 80% of your final grade.

Grade for the group—80% of the grade:

- Topic
    - Is the topic suitable for focus group research?
    - Is the topic relevant for the participants?
    - Is the topic ethical?

- The topic guide
    - How likely is the topic guide to foster conversation?
    - Does the topic guide follow conventions of good focus group interviewing?
    - Is the topic approached in a manner that is ethical?
    - Does the topic guide show sufficient knowledge of the topic?

- Prompts
    - How suitable and creative are the prompts that are used?

- Was the focus group successfully recorded?
- Is the informed consent documentation appropriate for the topic?
- How well does the group work together in creating the materials?

Individual component of the grade—20% of the grade:

- Engagement in the exercise
- Participation in all the elements of the exercise (planning, the actual focus group, and the discussion after)
- Contribution to the discussion after the focus group by methodological reflections or by analyzing the data

Exploring the Focus Group Method: A Practical Experience	*Worksheet*

This exercise consists of four phases: (1) planning, (2) the development of materials, (3) taking part in a focus group, and (4) discussing the experience.

1. PLANNING

In your group, choose a topic that is relevant to your focus group participants, that is, your peers.

- Exploring experiences of being a student at your college/university, living at your college/university, how students view your college/university
- Exploring a particular program, service, or ritual at your college/university
- Exploring the perceptions of students at your college/university about a relevant topic (e.g., dating, parties, workload, stress, media, social media, sports)

Remember that your participants are your fellow students. Usually, the group composition of a focus group is tied to the topic and the aims of a research project. In this class exercise, however, the selection of participants is already decided. Remember also that your participants need to have sufficient knowledge of the topic that is discussed.

Is it ethical?

- What kinds of ethical issues should be kept in mind in relation to exploring the topic? Is the topic suitable for a focus group setting?
- Are there any taboos that are relevant?
- Prepare appropriate informed consent documentation keeping in mind that in focus groups, confidentiality of the material cannot easily be guarded.

2. MATERIALS

Develop a topic guide.

- What kinds of questions would be most likely to generate meaningful discussion?
- What kinds of prompts could be used to invite discussion (leaflets, pictures, vignettes, newspaper headings, statements, quotes, video clips, music, poetry, webpages)?

The focus group should be recorded.

- You should test the equipment.

Two volunteers from your group will facilitate your focus group with another group of students:

- One primary facilitator who focuses the group and one observer facilitator who ensures that the technical side works

3. FOCUS GROUPS IN PRACTICE

On the day, bring your instructor a detailed copy of your topic guide:

- Include explanation on the prompts used, a description of the room layout, and details of practicalities (who is responsible for what)
- Include an example of your informed consent documentation

Set up the room in a way that is suitable.

- What kind of set up would best foster conversation?
- The facilitator might want to write on the chalkboard or flip chart or show a video clip.

Run a focus group or act as a focus group participant—60 minutes:

- Group 1 with facilitators from Group 3, room TBC
- Group 2 with facilitators from Group 1, room TBC
- Group 3 with facilitators from Group 2, room TBC

Use these guidelines for focus group participants.

- For this exercise, you are welcome to speak as yourself or to develop an alternative persona solely for the purposes of the exercise.
- Remember that this is a class setting and, as such, the confidentiality of your comments cannot be guaranteed.

4. DISCUSSION

The class following the focus groups is reserved for discussing the focus group methods, your experiences, and findings:

- Reporting back on the experience
- Discussing findings and the usefulness of focus group methodology
- Thinking of useful sociological concepts to analyze the material

OVERVIEW

This assignment is designed to expose you to active interviewing techniques. The active interview is a process where the interviewer and interviewee co-construct knowledge through a series of questions and answers. Your task is to select a topic of interest, develop an interview guide, interview respondents, and analyze your findings.

The learning objectives of this assignment are as follows:

1. Practice developing an interview guide

2. Learn through asking questions and listening

3. Gain confidence leading an active interview

4. Sharpen quantitative analytic skills

5. Understand the importance of reflexivity

INSTRUCTIONS

Pick a topic that is of interest to you. Examples could include topics such as the role of money in sports, the role of technology in political elections, or attitudes toward a specific social policy. Next, think of four potential people who may be knowledgeable about that topic. After completing these steps, follow the instructions below:

1. Create an interview guide of approximately 10 questions. These questions should be general in nature. The more specific the question, the more you are limiting the scope of the research. Your instructor will go over an example of an interview guide with you in class. Be prepared to share your interview guide with your peers.

2. Write a reflexive memo of one to two pages. Detail how you think that you, the researcher, will influence the interview process. Consider things such as your sensitivities to the topic you select and your relationship with the interview participants. Reflect on how your personality may guide your interviewing style.

3. Formally invite your four participants to be a part of this research project. You may connect with the individuals in person, over e-mail, or via telephone. When extending the invitation,

explain that you are conducting research for a class. Briefly, describe the topic that you are investigating, as well as approximately how long the interview will last. Please consult your instructor to find out what the desired interview length time is.

4. Schedule the four interviews. When doing so, space out each interview such that you have adequate time to digest the information from each interaction. Do not schedule interviews back-to-back. A 48 hour reflection time is recommended.

5. Conduct your first interview. In the spirit of the active interview process, do not be highly rigid in sticking to your interview guide. Instead, see where the conversation takes you. Use your instincts in determining if your participant is straying too far from the topic.

6. As quickly as possible after conducting the interview, write your interview notes. Detail the time, place, and atmosphere of your interview. Write down the key themes discussed by the participant, as well as how you felt throughout the course of the interaction. Also, detail any nonverbal communication cues that you observed during the interview.

7. Repeat Steps 5 and 6 with the remainder of your participants. Take time to reflect on each interview. What things went well? How can you improve your interviewing skills, thus moving forward?
What themes have been repeated between your participants?

8. After completing your four interviews, write a three- to four-page analysis. This analysis should detail

   a. the things that you learned about conducting interviews,

   b. major themes that arose from your interviews,

   c. your most surprising or unexpected findings,

   c. ways that this project helped you improve your interviewing skills.

GRADING CRITERIA

You will be assessed based on your performance on the following measures:

1. Interview guide (worth 20%)
   - Are the questions relevant to the topic?
   - Do the questions flow well?

2. Interview notes (worth 20%)
   - Are the time, place, atmosphere of the interview adequately detailed?
   - Are major themes discussed?

3. Analysis (worth 40%)
   - Does the paper discuss what you learned about conducting interviews?
   - Does the paper offer insight into the major themes of the interviews?
   - Is the paper thoughtful?

4. Reflexive memo (worth 20%)
   - Does this memo detail how you influence the interview process?
   - Is it thoughtful?

CHAPTER 6

QUANTITATIVE ANALYSIS

A fter conducting research, the social science researcher is left with a large amount of data. The crucial step is taking these data and analyzing them and then coming up with conclusions. The purpose of deductive research is to try to support a hypothesis in an effort to answer a research question. Hidden within the raw data collected are the relationships between the tested variables that, with the proper techniques can yield scientific support for a hypothesis or, equally importantly, scientific support for a **null hypothesis**. The techniques for ordering and understanding these data are covered in this chapter, as well as an exploration of the predictive powers of properly analyzed data sets.

In testing the relationship between the independent and dependent variables, the social science researcher is trying to determine whether the independent variable has any statistically significant impact on the dependent variable. The phrase "statistically significant" is important, and there are equations for determining it. Before you can determine if a relationship is significant, you have to analyze the data. One useful analytical tool is the cross-tabulation table, which will reveal any significant correlations and relationships between variables.

For the advanced research methods student, data analyzing can go beyond drawing conclusions about relationships between variables in data sets to using those conclusions to attempt to predict future events. Researchers using **regression** equations may look at the past and use data sets to place hard percentages on the effect the past has on the future. In the case of this book, that involves looking at the performance of two football teams for a number of key factors (points allowed, points scored, etc.) and attempting to scientifically determine the likelihood of these factors influencing the result of a Monday night football game.

In the end, the purpose of quantitative analysis is not to prove or disprove a hypothesis. The social science researcher never proves anything; the individual demonstrates a statistically significant relationship between key variables that supports a hypothesis. The distinction is important because in and of itself, the analysis demonstrates the importance of language and of not overstating one's results.

TURNING PEOPLE INTO PETRI DISHES! USING RANDOM ASSIGNMENT TO CREATE EQUIVALENT TEST GROUPS

Robert J. Youmans, PhD

George Mason University

OVERVIEW

Students do not always think that biology and other so-called hard sciences have very much in common with social science research. There is just something really "scientific looking" about a microscope or rack of test tubes, and social scientists rarely dress in white laboratory coats anymore. But stereotypical appearances aside, social sciences often employ many of the same research methods and logical assumptions used in biology, physics, and chemistry. Imagine a biologist who is trying to test what the optimal amount of sunlight is for growing a particular microorganism. She might start by obtaining some samples of the microorganism and then expose each sample to different levels of sunlight. After a period of time, one sample might grow larger than the others, indicating to the scientist what the optimal level of sunlight is for that microorganism.

Like biologists, social scientists often want to know how a variable is affecting people, but social scientists face one major obstacle that is not often found in other fields of science: They don't have petri dishes! Although this may sound more like the punch line to a bad science joke, think about it for a minute; the biologist we imagined before would never think of testing different levels of light on different strains of the microorganisms in different containers; she would want the strains of the microorganism and the conditions of the test to be identical for each of her samples so that she could attribute changes in her samples to the sunlight alone. But ensuring that each condition in an experiment starts out the same can be a real problem for social scientists because they rarely have identical people to create identical samples from. In fact, during a typical social science experiment, all sorts of different people show up to participate. How then can a social scientist be sure that differences in a dependent variable are due to the independent variable they manipulated? What methods can they use to make sure that the groups of people in the different conditions of an experiment are all the same before the test begins?

Turning People Into Petri Dishes! Using Random Assignment to Create Equivalent Test Groups	Worksheet

Instructions *for Step 1 of the Activity: Carefully answer each of the following survey questions either in the space below or on the provided index card. Be sure not to put your name on this sheet or the card so that your answers remain anonymous!*

Response to Question 1:

Response to Question 2:

Response to Question 3:

Response to Question 4:

Response to Question 5:

	Turning People Into Petri Dishes! Using Random Assignment to Create Equivalent Test Groups	Worksheet

Instructions for Step 2 of the Activity: Follow along with the rest of the class as the average group responses to each of the survey questions are reported when the data reported is from 5, 10, or 20 randomly assigned survey responses. Note that as more people are randomly assigned to a group, the two groups will become more or less equivalent on their average responses to each of the survey questions.

	Average Responses Group 5A	Average Responses Group 5B	Average Responses Group 10A	Average Responses Group 10B	Average Responses Group 20A	Average Responses Group 20B
Survey Question 1						
Survey Question 2						
Survey Question 3						
Survey Question 4						
Survey Question 5						

A few follow-up questions to think about include these:

1. Would a group of randomly selected college students' responses become equal to a group of randomly selected responses from an elder care facility or an elementary school? Why or why not?

2. You often hear that a study has more "power" if the experiments that were conducted were on more people. How might the idea of power be related to the ability of random assignment to equate two groups of people that are drawn from a larger population?

3. The metaphor of petri dishes that is used in biology was used in this experiment, but even on a petri dish there are sometimes contaminants or other factors that may unintentionally skew the results of a single study. What could a social scientist do to build confidence that the results of a single study are correct?

CROSS-TABULATION TABLES AND THE RELATIONSHIPS BETWEEN VARIABLES

Anne Kristen Hunter

University of North Carolina at Chapel Hill

OVERVIEW

This is an exercise in building cross-tabulation tables from a raw data set. The activity will give you a hands-on feel for assembling and interpreting quantitative data. Whenever you collect data, you will go through a similar process, either by hand or assisted by computer software. This activity will also give you the chance to practice interpreting causal relationships and to see how introducing a third variable can influence our understanding of an original bivariate relationship.

INSTRUCTIONS

The mock data used for this activity comes from a fictional class survey of an upper division class in economic sociology. Each student in the class was assigned a random number for identification purposes (ID).

Students were coded for their gender (SEX), and the class contained both men (M) and women (F). Students were asked their class year in college (CLASS). Because it was an upper division course, only third-year (JUNIOR) and fourth-year (SENIOR) students were present. Next students were asked their major. Because of the class topic, both sociology (SOCI) and economics (ECON) students were enrolled.

Students were also asked to report about their drinking habits (DRINK). Students could report that they had consumed alcoholic beverages on the previous weekend (DRINK) or that they had not (NOT DRINK). Finally, students were asked about their job aspirations (JOB). Some students reported wanting careers with for-profit businesses (PRIVATE), while others reported wanting to work in the nonprofit or public sectors (PUBLIC).

You will first make a table of the frequency distributions of your variables. Second, you will make a bivariate cross tab of your dependent and independent variables. You will need to write out an interpretation of the relationship in that cross-tab table. Third, you will make a **multivariate** cross tab of your dependent, independent, and control variables. You will again need to interpret the relationships among these variables.

Remember to use percentage down the columns so that each column totals to 100%.

The first relationship you will consider treats drinking as the dependent variable and gender as the independent. Since this relationship may also be affected by age, you will include class year as your control variable. For the second relationship, you will treat job aspiration as the dependent variable, and gender will again be your independent variable. You will control for academic major.

GRADING

Your grade for this activity will be calculated out of 12 points. You will receive one point each for the tables and one point each for your interpretations.

Cross-Tabulation Tables and The Relationships Between Variables	Worksheet

Frequency Distributions of Drinking, Gender, and Class Year

Dependent:		Independent:		Control:	
y1:	%	x1:	%	z1:	%
y2:	%	x2:	%	z2:	%
	100%		100%		100%

Cross-Tabulation of Drinking and Gender

Dependent Variable:	Independent Variable:		TOTAL
	x1:	x2:	
y1:	% N =	% N =	% N =
y2:	% N =	% N =	% N =
TOTAL	% N =	% N =	100% N = 50

1. What is the relationship between drinking and gender?

Cross-Tabulation of Drinking, Gender, and Class Year

Dependent Variable:	Control Variable:				TOTAL
	z1:		z2:		
	Independent Variable:				
	x1:	x2:	x1:	x2:	
y1:	% N =	% N =	% N =	% N =	% N =
y2:	% N =	% N =	% N =	% N =	% N =
TOTAL	% N =	% N =	% N =	% N =	100% N = 50

1. What is the relationship between gender and drinking, holding class year constant?

2. What is the relationship between class year and drinking, holding gender constant?

Frequency Distributions of Job Aspiration, Gender, and College Major

Dependent:		Independent:		Control:	
y1:	%	x1:	%	z1:	%
y2:	%	x2:	%	z2:	%
	100%		100%		100%

Cross-Tabulation of Job Aspiration and Gender

	Independent Variable:		
Dependent Variable:	x1:	x2:	TOTAL
y1:	% N =	% N =	% N =
y2:	% N =	% N =	% N =
TOTAL	% N =	% N =	100% N = 50

1. What is the relationship between job aspiration and gender?

Cross-Tabulation of Job Aspiration, Gender, and College Major

Dependent Variable:	Control Variable:				TOTAL
	z1:		z2:		
	Independent Variable:				
	x1:	x2:	x1:	x2:	
y1:	% N =	% N =	% N =	% N =	% N =
y2:	% N =	% N =	% N =	% N =	% N =
TOTAL	% N =	% N =	% N =	% N =	100% N = 50

1. What is the relationship between gender and job aspiration, holding major constant?

2. What is the relationship between major and job aspiration, holding gender constant?

ID	SEX	CLASS	MAJOR	DRINK	JOB
01	F	Junior	Soci	Not Drink	Private
02	F	Senior	Econ	Drink	Private
03	M	Senior	Econ	Drink	Private
04	F	Senior	Soci	Not Drink	Public
05	F	Junior	Econ	Not Drink	Public
06	M	Junior	Soci	Not Drink	Private
07	M	Junior	Econ	Not Drink	Private
08	M	Junior	Econ	Drink	Public
09	F	Junior	Soci	Not Drink	Public
10	M	Senior	Econ	Not Drink	Private
11	F	Junior	Econ	Drink	Private
12	M	Junior	Econ	Drink	Public
13	M	Junior	Soci	Drink	Private
14	F	Senior	Soci	Drink	Public
15	M	Junior	Soci	Not Drink	Public
16	F	Senior	Soci	Drink	Private
17	F	Senior	Econ	Drink	Public
18	M	Junior	Econ	Not Drink	Private
19	F	Junior	Soci	Drink	Public
20	M	Senior	Soci	Drink	Private
21	F	Senior	Soci	Not Drink	Private
22	F	Junior	Econ	Drink	Private
23	F	Senior	Soci	Drink	Public
24	F	Junior	Soci	Drink	Private
25	M	Junior	Econ	Not Drink	Private

ID	SEX	CLASS	MAJOR	DRINK	JOB
26	M	Junior	Econ	Not Drink	Private
27	F	Junior	Soci	Not Drink	Public
28	M	Junior	Soci	Drink	Private
29	M	Senior	Econ	Drink	Private
30	F	Senior	Econ	Drink	Private
31	M	Senior	Econ	Drink	Private
32	F	Senior	Soci	Drink	Private
33	F	Senior	Soci	Drink	Public
34	M	Senior	Soci	Drink	Public
35	M	Senior	Econ	Drink	Private
36	F	Junior	Econ	Not Drink	Private
37	M	Junior	Soci	Drink	Public
38	F	Senior	Econ	Drink	Private
39	M	Junior	Econ	Drink	Private
40	M	Junior	Soci	Not Drink	Private
41	M	Senior	Econ	Drink	Public
42	F	Senior	Econ	Drink	Private
43	F	Junior	Econ	Drink	Public
44	M	Senior	Soci	Not Drink	Private
45	M	Senior	Soci	Drink	Public
46	F	Senior	Soci	Drink	Public
47	F	Junior	Soci	Drink	Public
48	M	Junior	Econ	Drink	Private
49	F	Senior	Soci	Drink	Public
50	F	Senior	Econ	Not Drink	Public

OVERVIEW

This exercise is an illustration of hypothesis testing with *t* statistic. This exercise will test your knowledge of *t* tests and hypotheses testing and effect size measures. You will generate, analyze, and interpret the data. You will also learn how to use Statistical Package for the Social Sciences (SPSS) statistical package, interpret SPSS output, and describe the results in American Psychological Association (APA) format.

INSTRUCTIONS

There are three steps to completing this assignment:

Step 1: Taking the survey

Everyone in class completes an anonymous Student Survey for the *t* Test Exercise

Step 2: Entering the data into SPSS

All answers all collected and the data are combined and entered into SPSS. Make sure to correctly label the variables.

Step 3: Data analysis and interpretation

The data set is analyzed using SPSS statistical package. Use the provided worksheet to report your answers and record your interpretations of the results. See the provided handout for SPSS and APA style instructions.

| **Student Survey for the t Test Exercise** | **Worksheet** |

Please answer the four questions below.

Do not sign your name

1. How tall are you? Convert feet into inches.

   I am _____inches tall.

2. What is your gender? Check one.

   Male _____   Female _____

3. On average, how many **minutes per typical week** do you spend studying for your research methods course outside of class? Convert hours into minutes.

   In a typical week, I study _____minutes.

4. In your opinion, how many **minutes a week** *should* you spend studying for your research methods course outside of class to be able to earn an A?

   I should study _____minutes to earn an A in this class.

Student Survey for the t Test Exercise	*Worksheet*

Study I: Human height is highly variable but normally falls within a certain range. Most adults obtain their full height around their late teens.

The average height for male adults in America is about 5 feet 9 inches to 5 feet 10 inches.

For female adults in America, the average height is 5 feet 3 inches to 5 feet 8 inches. Overall, adult population mean height is: 67.5 inches.

Source: http://encyclopedia.thefreedictionary.com/Human%20height

A sample of adult individuals (n = _____) is selected from a population with a mean height of $\mu = 67.5$ inches, and their heights are recorded.

Does this sample accurately represent the population of American adults as a whole?

Use a two-tailed test and **alpha level** of 0.05.

Run the analysis in SPSS and answer the following questions:

1. What kind of a *t* test should you use?

2. Explain why

3. What is the test value? $\mu =$

4. What is the sample mean $M =$

5. What is the sample **standard deviation**? $SD =$

6. What is the obtained *t*? $t =$

7. What are the degrees of freedom? $df =$

8. Is the *t* statistically significant?

9. What is the exact probability of **Type I error**?

10. Compute Cohen's d $d =$

Interpret and describe the results in APA style. Make sure to include all appropriate statistics:

Study II. A sample of college women (n = __) and men (n = __) is selected from the general population. Their heights are recorded.

Is there a statistically significant height difference between the two groups? Using SPSS, conduct a *t* test and report your results. Use a two-tailed test and alpha level of 0.05.

1.   What kind of a *t* test should you use?

2.   Explain why

3.   What is the sample mean for women? $M =$

4.   What is the sample standard deviation for women? $SD =$

5.   What is the sample mean for men? $M =$

6.   What is the sample standard deviation for men? $SD =$

7. What is the obtained *t*? $t =$

8. What are the degrees of freedom? $df =$

9. Is the *t* statistically significant?

10. What is the exact probability of Type I error?

11. Compute the effect size $r^2 =$

Interpret and describe the results in APA style. Make sure to include all appropriate statistics:

Study III. A college Research Methods class instructor is interested in finding out whether her students spend enough time each week on independent study. College students enrolled in a psychology course ($n =$ ___) were selected from the general college population. Each student reported the number of minutes he or she spent studying for the research methods course during a typical week. Each student also provided his or her estimate of the number of minutes needed to get an A in the class.

Was there significant difference between the study time actually spent studying and the study time needed to earn an A? Using SPSS, conduct a t test and report your results.

Use a two-tailed test and alpha level of 0.05.

1. What kind of t test did you use?

2. Explain why

3. What was the sample mean? $M =$

4. What was the sample standard deviation? $SD =$

5. What was the obtained *t*?   *t* =

6. What were the degrees of freedom?   *df* =

7. Is the *t* statistically significant?

8. What is the exact probability of Type I error?

9. Compute the effect size r^2 =

Interpret and describe the results in APA format. Make sure to include all appropriate statistics:

Student Survey for the t Test Exercise	T Test Activity Handout

1. Using SPSS to analyze the results, follow these steps:
   - ☐ Start
   - ☐ Programs
   - ☐ SPSS for Windows
   - ☐ Open the **t test** activity data file
   - ☐ Click Analyze on the tool bar
   - ☐ Select Compare Means
   - ☐ Select the appropriate test
   - ☐ One-sample *t* test: highlight and click over the name of the test variable; enter the hypothesized value for the population mean into the Test Value box
   - ☐ Independent-samples *t* test: highlight and click over the name of the test variable; highlight and click over the name of the grouping variable; define groups (enter 1 and 2 for specified values)
   - ☐ Paired-samples *t* test: highlight and click over the names of the paired variables
   - ☐ Click OK

2. Report the results of a *t* test according to the APA style.

The results of each experiment should be described in terms of the variables and the test statistics. The description should make clear what variables (if any) were manipulated, what **test statistics** were obtained, and what the results were of the statistical analysis.

In addition to clearly stating the *t* test conclusions, you should always report the following:

- Sample mean(s) (*M*)
- Sample standard deviation(s) (*SD*)
- Obtained *t* statistic and *df*
- Alpha level (e.g., p < .05 or p > .05 depending on the outcome)
- And, finally, the effect size

EXAMPLE 1: The single-sample *t* test

The subjects' task completion time averaged $M = 36$ minutes with $SD = 3$. Statistical analysis indicated that they spent significantly less time than would be expected by chance, $t(8) = 6.00, p < .05, r^2 = 81.82\%$.

EXAMPLE 2: Independent-measures *t* test

The group taking the supplement recalled more words ($M = 26, SD = 4.71$) than the group that did not take supplements ($M = 18, SD = 4.22$). This difference was statistically significant, $t(18) = 4.00, p < .05, d = 1.79$.

EXAMPLE 3: Repeated-measures *t* test

Meditation reduced the number of doses of medication needed to control insomnia by an average of $M = 2.00$ with $SD = 1.00$. The reduction was statistically significant, $t(4) = 4.47$, $p < .05, r^2 = 0.83$.

EFFECT SIZE EQUATIONS

Independent samples	Single sample	Related samples
$d = \dfrac{M_1 - M_2}{\sqrt{s^2}_p}$	$d = \dfrac{M - \mu}{s}$ $r^2 = \dfrac{t^2}{t^2 + df}$	$d = \dfrac{M_D}{s}$

REGRESSION: CAN IT DETERMINE THE WINNER OF MONDAY NIGHT'S GAME?

Lisa A. Cave

Morehead State University

OVERVIEW

The purpose of this assignment is to help you think critically about regression and its results. The text here refers to the 2009 Patriots-Saints *Monday Night Football* game and should be adjusted accordingly. You will need to substitute the teams playing in the game specific to your course for this assignment. Your instructor will assist you with this and will provide you with the raw data necessary to complete the assignment.

On Monday night is the highly publicized game between the Patriots and the Saints; you have been provided with two regressions, one for each team, that **may** be used to predict each team's possibility of winning—based on the regression results provided you are asked to predict which team will win. The assignment provides the summary statistics and a description of each variable included in the estimation.

The first purpose of this assignment is to help you become familiar with the presentation of summary statistics and regression results. As students who may plan to continue in graduate studies or work in government, you should be familiar with these tables and what they represent.

The second goal of this assignment is for you to think critically about regression results. You are asked to make a prediction about the winner of the football game based on the regressions provided. At this point in the course, we have covered multiple regression and regression output. You should be able to look at the estimation results, determine the overall predictive value, and identify and discuss the meaning of each variable in terms of magnitude and statistical significance.

In addition, we have also discussed some of the underlying assumptions of regression and under what circumstances regression results may not be valid. Based on what you know about the assumptions of multiple regressions, you should be able to identify those issues that would invalidate the regression results such as underspecified models, **multicollinearity**, and endogeneity.

INSTRUCTIONS

- You instructor will provide you with two regression equations, one for the Saints and one for the Patriots. The regressions contain information about all regular season games that each team played prior to Monday night's game since the beginning of the 2007 season.
- Take about 10 to 15 minutes to look at the information provided.

- Pick a winner for the football game on Monday night and then answer and submit the three questions on the last page.
- You may discuss the results and questions with other students, friends, and family.

The following equation is estimated for both the Saints and the Patriots where each observation represents one of the 42 weeks since the beginning of the 2007 season up to the Monday night game:

$$Win_t = Home_t + Opponent_t + Monday_t + Total\ Yards_t + Total\ Yards\ Defense_t + Year_t + Week_t + e_t$$

- *Win* represents whether the team won or not. It is equal to 1 if the Patriots or Saints won that week and equal to 0 if the Patriots or Saints lost.
- *Home* represents whether the Patriots or Saints were at home = 1 or away = 0.
- *Opponent* represents the Entertainment and Sports Programming Network (ESPN) power ranking for the Patriots or Saints opponent prior to the game.
- *Monday* is equal to 1 if the game was a Monday night game and 0 otherwise.
- *Total Yards* are the total number of yards that the Patriots or Saints gained.
- *Total Yards Defense* is the total number of yards that the Patriots or Saints defense gave up.
- *Year* is the year that the game was played.
- *Week* is the week that the game was played.
- *e* is the error term.

Below are the expected impacts of each variable on the possibility of a win.

- Home: We can expect this variable to be positive since there may be a home field advantage effect.
- Opponent: Since the ranking of an opponent goes from low to high—where the lower the ranking, the better the opponent. We can expect this variable to be negative—the better the opponent, the less likely the probability that the team will win.
- Monday: It represents whether it's a Monday night game or not. We can expect this variable to be positive—teams sometimes play better in Monday night games.
- Total yards: This represents the total yards that the team gained during the game—total rushing plus total passing yards. We can expect this variable to be positive. The more yards a team gains, the more likely they are to score and possibly win.
- Total yards defense: This represents the total number of yards that the opponent gained during the game. This is expected to be negative. The higher the number of yards an opponent has, the more likely they are to score and possibly win.
- Year: This is the year that the game was played between 2007 and 2009.
- Week: This is the week, 1 through 17, that the game was played in.

Summary Statistics

	Variable	Observations	Mean	Std. Dev.	Min.	Max.
Patriots						
	Win	42	0.810	0.397	0	1
	Home Game	42	0.524	0.505	0	1
	Opponent Ranking	42	17.143	9.734	1	32
	Total Yards	42	395	88	215	619
	Total Yards Defense	42	298	75	168	461
	Year	42	2008	1	2007	2009
	Week	42	8.333	4.887	1	17
	Monday	42	0.095	0.297	0	1
Saints						
	Win	42	0.595	0.497	0	1
	Home Game	42	0.500	0.506	0	1
	Opponent Ranking	42	17.976	9.256	2	32
	Total Yards	42	394	75	246	538
	Total Yards Defense	42	341	83	195	478
	Year	42	2008	1	2007	2009
	Week	42	8.429	4.865	1	17
	Monday	42	0.119	0.328	0	1

Regression Results for the Patriots and Saints

Win	Patriots	Saints
Home	0.06 (0.11)	0.18 (0.14)
Ranking	0.01 (0.01)	0.02*
Total Yards	0.001 (0.001)	0.001***
Total Yards Defense	0.002** (0.001)	0.0001 (0.001)
Year	−0.14* (0.07)	0.19** (0.09)
Week	0.01 (0.01)	0.004 (0.01)
Monday	0.21 (0.18)	−0.05 (0.21)
Constant	279.08* (139.86)	−378.71** (186.99)
Adjusted R² **Observations**	0.28 42	0.28 42

NOTES

1. The coefficients are the top figures, and the standard errors are shown in parentheses underneath their respective coefficients.

2. A * represents if the coefficient is significant at the 10% level; ** if the coefficient is significant at the 5% level; and *** if the coefficient is significant at the 1% level.

Regression: Can It Determine the Winner of Monday Night's Game?	Worksheet

The assignment is worth 20 points. Please answer the following questions before kickoff on Monday night. You should write in a clear, logical fashion, and you may use bullet points. Grading will be based not on whether you predicted the outcome of the game correctly but what factors you base your decision on.

1. Who will win the football game? The Patriots or Saints?

2. After examining the summary statistics and regression results, consider the following questions:

   2.1. Describe the overall predictive value of the estimation (*hint: R^2 and what this value means*) (2 points).

   2.2. Identify the importance of the variables in terms of statistical significance, direction, and magnitude (8 points).

   2.3. Did you use the regression results to help you determine the winner of Monday night's game? Yes or No (1 point).

3. Do you have any reservations about using the regressions above to predict the winner of the football game? In particular, consider each of the following issues, provide a definition, determine whether the issue exists in the estimation, and in what way:

   3.1 Underspecified model (3 points)

   3.2 Multicollinearity (3 points)

   3.3 Endogeneity (3 points)

CHAPTER 7

MIXED METHODS
AND TRIANGULATION

The social science researcher has to be able to use all of the tools in this book and sometimes use all of them in the same research project. **Triangulation** is using more than one method to approach a research question: interview, survey, observational. Sometimes, the best way to fully understand a research topic is to use them all.

This chapter offers two full semester-long projects, incorporating elements from all of our earlier chapters, as well as an activity that explores comparative historical research using archival documents, which are an important way for researchers to understand events in the past from multiple perspectives. This activity involves investigating an event at your school using documents from your school archives to provide a nuanced and multifaceted view of the event.

One of the semester-long projects is an ethnographic research project, and for those of you interested in anthropology, it provides an invaluable guide going from picking a community to study to presenting a research project in the same way the professionals do. Anthropology is an important and exciting discipline within social science, and new anthropologists are always needed to unlock the secrets of human societies both ancient and modern.

This is the final chapter in the book, and with its completion, you're an important step closer to being a social science researcher! Some of the skills may have been difficult to learn, some may have been frustrating to learn, but don't let that deter you from future study in research methods. Using these skills, you can become part of a group of researchers committed to understanding the most perplexing subject of all: ourselves.

EXPLORING CAMPUS HISTORY

Mikaila Mariel Lemonik Arthur

Rhode Island College

OVERVIEW

This assignment will give you the opportunity to explore a series of documents from the archives at your campus. It will give you a taste of what the process of comparative-historical research drawing on archival documents as a datum source is like. These documents will serve as the basis of a short research project in which you will synthesize the information each contains to develop a series of findings about your campus at a particular point in time.

This assignment will help you meet several learning objectives in your research methods course. First of all, it will give you the chance to learn how to use archival datum sources to draw conclusions about particular social contexts in particular times and places. Secondly, it will enable you to practice using inductive research techniques to generate theory from data. Finally, it will show you how triangulation is used to strengthen conclusions by using multiple datum sources that each speak to a similar theme.

INSTRUCTIONS

Your instructor will provide you with a series of archival documents. Begin by examining each document and answering the five questions on the first section of the worksheet for each one of the five documents. Then, taking the group of documents as a whole, answer the three questions in the second section of the worksheet. Finally, drawing on the notes you have taken on the first two pages of the worksheet, develop a sociological argument that would serve as the basis for further investigation into the experiences of your college campus.

Once this is completed, you will develop a sociological argument based on these documents. You might compare the campus of the past with the campus of today, you might discuss social changes occurring on campus in the time period during which the documents were written, or you might find another issue that jumps out at you in the documents. Please write about one page laying out a sociological research question and as much as you can of an exploration of it based on what you have learned from the documents provided. You must rely on at least three of the documents to make your case, using proper citations to document your evidence. You should conclude with a summary of what else you would need to know in order to make your case stronger and what sources and research methods you would use to find that information.

GRADING

This assignment will be graded based on the following criteria:

- Submission of a complete worksheet that includes answers to all of the assigned questions
- Accurate summary of the data contained in each archival document
- Accurate synthesis of the group of documents to draw inferences about the college campus at the time covered in the documents
- Development of a sociological argument based on findings from the documents that include appropriate and clearly documented evidence from the documents
- Appropriate suggestions for further research that outline the research questions to be pursued and the data's sources to be located if such a project were undertaken

Exploring Campus History	*Worksheet*

Group Members' Names:

Your group has been given a selection of documents from the campus archives. The first step is to review the documents that you have been provided with, answering the following questions.

1. When, where, and by whom was this document written?

2. Who is the intended audience for this document?

3. What observations do you have about the style, format, or content of this document?

4. What do you think might have been omitted from this document?

5. What does this document tell you about your campus at the time that the document was written?

The second step is to bring these documents together and consider them as a whole.

1. Taking all these documents together, what would you say your campus was like at the time the documents were written? How does it differ from your campus today?

2. What sorts of changes had the campus recently undergone when these documents were created?

3. How are the stories told by these documents similar from or different from one another?

OVERVIEW

This assignment is a semester-long group project, which will give you the opportunity to practically apply your quantitative research skills. Early in the semester, you will be assigned to a study and working group that consists of four individuals. Over the course of the semester, each group will be expected to draft an original questionnaire, solicit 40 respondents to their survey (i.e., 10 per student) and perform three exercises with their data (i.e., respectively, one exercise on descriptive statistics, means testing and correlation, and regression analysis).

Assignment 1: Drafting a questionnaire and creating a data set

Think of an interesting social science topic of your choice (be creative). Specify the dependent variable as a continuous variable, and think of six to eight independent (explanatory) variables, which might affect the dependent variable. You must include three types of independent variables: continuous, ordinal, and dichotomous variables. Do not ask questions that are too sensitive.

Example questionnaire:

Dear participants

Please answer the following questions, which will be exclusively used for data analytical purposes in my political science research methods class. If you are not sure about an answer, then just give an estimate. All answers will be treated anonymously. I thank you for contributing to our study.

Dependent variable:

- How much money do you spend "going out" per week?

Independent variables:

- What is your gender?
- What is your year of study?
- On average, how many hours do you spend studying per week?
- On average, how often do you go partying per week?
- On a scale from 0 to 100, determine whether you can have fun without alcohol (0 meaning you can have a lot of fun, 100 you cannot have fun at all)?
- On a scale from 0 to 100, determine the quality of the officially sanctioned free-time activities at your institution (0 meaning they are horrible, 100 meaning they are very good)?
- What percentage of your tuition do you pay yourself?

It is imperative that you hand in a draft questionnaire before collecting your responses.

Upon my approval of your survey, solicit 40 responses (i.e., 10 per person) from fellow undergraduate students and input the data into a Statistical Package for the Social Sciences (SPSS) sheet. Make sure to code dummy variables (e.g., gender) zero and one. Code ordinal variables consecutively (e.g., for year of studies in the above example, assign the value 0 for freshman, 1 for sophomores, 2 for juniors, 3 for seniors, and 4 for super seniors).

For your first group presentation, you will present the questionnaire and the logic behind your topic. You should also justify why you included all the questions from which you derive your independent variables. Finally, comment on the relationship you expect to see between each independent variable and the dependent variable.

Assignment 2: Descriptive statistics

The second assignment will consist of five exercises:

1. Graph your dependent variable and one continuous independent variable as a box plot.

2. Graph one of your ordinal independent variables as a histogram.

3. Graph one of your ordinal independent variables as a pie chart.

4. Present some descriptive statistics of your dependent variable.

5. Present some frequency distribution of your dependent variable.

During your in-class presentation show and interpret the SPSS outputs. While doing so, you will need to cover both the statistical and substantive meaning of your descriptive analyses.

Assignment 3: Means testing and correlations

The third assignment will consist of three exercises:

1. Conduct an independent samples t test. Use the dependent variable of your study; as grouping variable, use one of your dichotomous variables.

2. Conduct a one way Analysis of Variance (ANOVA) test. Use the dependent variable of your study; as factor, use one of your ordinal variables.

3. Run a correlation matrix with all your continuous variables.

   During your in-class presentation, you will interpret the outputs and evaluate whether your test results make substantive sense.

Assignment 4: Regression analysis

1. Formulate hypotheses; state how you think each independent variable relates to the dependent variable.

2. Run a multivariate regression analysis with all your independent variables and your dependent variable.

3. Create an interaction term; include it in your regression analysis and interpret it.

   After you state your hypotheses make sure to thoroughly interpret the regression output during your group presentation. In particular, be sure to interpret the statistical and substantive meaning of all the explanatory variables, the standardized coefficients, and the overall model fit. Finally, shortly highlight how you think your model could be further refined (for example, think of variables that might be pertinent but which you did not include in your initial questionnaire).

OVERVIEW

In this ethnographic research project, you will engage in the **practice of ethnography**, including design, execution, analysis of data, and presentation of results. You will work in small groups on topics of your preference. The project consists of a series of individual and group exercises. Each project exercise represents a different stage of research: literature review; formative theory, goals, and project design; participant observation and fieldnotes; interviewing and transcription; analysis; conclusions and future research directions; and verbal and written presentations of results.

The two final exercises are a **group presentation** of results and **individual research papers** based on the projects. The project presentation is designed to encourage formal public speaking and to introduce you to the format and scope of academic research presentations. Each group will present their research findings in a conference-style presentation at the end of the semester. The individual research paper will be in the format of a professional research article in the social sciences (anthropology, sociology, psychology, etc.), to promote scholarly writing skills.

INSTRUCTIONS

Please see each individual exercise that follows for detailed instructions.

GRADING

For group exercises, the grade is determined by two components: overall group grade and average of team member assessment of individual performance. The overall group grade will be made by the professor; it will be scored up to 10. The professor will then average your percentage effort, as evaluated by other group members. The professor will then determine the individual final grade: group grade x average percentage effort. Grading criteria for each exercise will closely follow the required components and format of each exercise.

Ethnographic Research Project	*Worksheet*

Group Topic Identification and Literature Review

<u>EVERYONE MUST TURN IN TEAM MEMBER ASSESSMENT, TOO.</u>

****

Team Members:

Date:

****

Instructions. Using the format below, identify your research topic and then present your annotated bibliography. Each member must provide three articles (or book chapters from an edited
book). For your citations, put your initials next to the citation (anywhere noticeable is fine).

Remember that all citations must be from social science databases (e.g., AnthroSource or
Anthropological Literature), must be written no earlier than 1995, and must be articles or chapters in edited books.

Topic:

Annotated Bibliography

<u>For each citation and summary, use the following format:</u>

Last Name, First Name. (Year). Title of Article. ***Title of Journal*** **Volume (Issue):Page–page.**
   Summary: (For each summary, include research aims, population, methods, conclusions *in your own words*.). (Name of team member who wrote the summary)

Example:

Fleuriet, K. Jill. (2007). Articulating Distress on Multiple Levels: Illness, History, and Culture Among the Kumiai of Baja California, Mexico. *Mexican Studies/Estudios Mexicanos* 23(1):155–180. (Team member: KJF)
   Summary: Fleuriet's primary research aim was to explain the illness phenomenon of low/variable blood pressure among the Kumiai Indians in northern Baja California, Mexico. She used semistructured interviews, surveys, and participant observation. In the community, she interviewed Kumiai men and women who had had low/variable blood pressure. She also interviewed their most common health care providers, located in Ensenada. She lived in Ensenada and spent days in the Kumiai community. Her conclusion is that low/variable blood pressure is the embodiment of gender asymmetry, stress from being too poor or too rich, and kinship stress connected to changing power relations among Kumiai clans. (Jill Fleuriet)

****

Project Exercise 2

**Group Research Goal, Aims, Formative Theory,
and Basic Project Design**

EVERYONE MUST TURN IN TEAM MEMBER ASSESSMENT, TOO.

****

Team Members:

Date:

Topic:

****

Instructions for Research Goal and Aims. Using the format below, identify your research goals and two to three aims and explain how your research may contribute to relevant literature on this topic. Your Goal and Aims sections do not need to be in complete sentences, but your explanation of how the research will contribute to the literature must be in complete sentences. All answers must be TYPED.

Research Goal:

Research Aims (no more than three):

1.

2.

3.

Explanation of how this research will contribute to the literature on this topic:

****

Instructions for Formative Theory and Basic Project Design. Using the format below, present and explain your team's formative theory, unit of analysis with justification, selection criteria, recruitment procedure, design of participant observation with justification, and observation topic guide with justification. You may use more than the space provided, if necessary. *Answers must be TYPED and in complete sentences.*

Formative Theory:

Unit of Analysis and Justification for Unit of Analysis:

Selection Criteria:

Recruitment Procedure:

When, Where, and How of Participation Observation, With Justification:

Observations Topics, With Justification:

Interview Guide, Including Topics, Subtopics, and Prompts

Project Exercise 3:

Individual Team Member Participant Observation and Fieldnotes

Do the participant observation ***before*** the interview.

Exchange these fieldnotes with team members by the day this exercise is due

****

Your Name:

Date:

Team Members:

Topic:

Date/Time/Location of Participant Observation:

****

Instructions for Fieldnotes. Using the format below for fieldnotes, conduct **3 HOURS** of participant observation. The condensed account may be handwritten (but legible!); the expanded account and initial interpretations and analysis must be typed.

Date: **Time:**   **Location:**

Condensed Account (use as much space as needed)**:**

Expanded Account (use as much space as needed)**:**

Initial Interpretations/Analysis (use as much space as needed):

Project Exercise 4

Individual Team Member Interview and Transcription

Do the interview **after** the participant observation.

Exchange your transcript with team members by the day this exercise is due

****

Your Name:

Date:

Team Members:

Topic:

Date/Time/Location of Interview:

****

Revised Interview Guide, Including Topics, Subtopics, and Prompts (Using feedback from professor, revise and present here your final interview guide. Use as much space as necessary. It must be typed. It will be the same guide for every team member.)

Instructions for Interview. Using the topic guide developed by your group, interview **ONE PERSON**—this person must be 18 years or older, of sound mind, a friend or family member, and a member of the community you are studying. She or he must also agree to an audio recording of the transcript. Use the team-developed interview guide and *make sure* you ask every single question and cover every single topic.

If you do not have access to a digital recorder (most cell phones have a record function—be sure to check clarity beforehand), come see me.

Once you have finished the interview, you will transcribe the interview. There is free software to facilitate transcribing: http://www.nch.com.au/scribe/

NOTE: Plan ample time for transcribing. For a skilled transcriptionist, it takes 3 hours to transcribe 1 hour of interview. Note also, you will be graded on how well you covered the interview topics. Lastly, exchange transcripts with other team members.

Transcript (Use as much space as necessary. It must be typed.)

Project Exercise 5
Individual Team Member Analysis and Results
****

Your Name:

Date:

Team Members:

Topic:

****

INSTRUCTIONS. Individually review the team's fieldnotes and transcripts, using grounded theory. Following the format below, present the results of your analysis, including themes, subthemes, examples from interview, observations, and any archival materials for each theme and subtheme, and interpretation of your data. List and/or explain as many themes as you found in your analysis. Answers must be TYPED. <u>Exchange your analysis with other team members by the day this exercise is due</u>.

Theme: *"Girl foods"*

Example from interview: *"They say you're supposed to eat salads and s**t if you're a girl, but I don't. I eat steaks, drink beer. But, if I had to say what foods are that women are supposed to eat, I'd say salads, low-cal, low-fat, at least in public."*

Example from observation: *Out of 10 women, 8 women bought nonsalad, supposedly high calorie foods, such as hamburgers and fries. Of these 8, six finished their meals and also had dessert.*

Example from archival materials: *In the 3(1) issue of the* Paesano, *one ad for a steakhouse had men eating, and women were talking. One ad for a sub shop had both men and women eating subs.*

Subtheme A: *Women who eat "girl foods" are perceived to be overly concerned with their weight.*

Example from interview: *"I think girls who eat salads all the time are making a statement or are freaked out about their weight. I don't think it's about making a statement or anything."*

Example from observation: The women who bought salads tended to sit with other women who bought salads. They talked about their food and weight more than women who did not buy salads.

Example from archival materials: In the 3(2) issue of the Paesano, an ad for weight loss contained no men, only one woman who was eating a salad and smiling.

Subtheme B (repeat as many times as necessary): Men who eat "girl foods" eat alone or are ridiculed by friends.

Example from interview: "If I ate a salad for lunch? My friends would make fun of me. I could have a salad and a steak, though, that'd be ok. It's stupid, though."

Example from observation: No men were observed eating salads.

Example from archival materials: Of the five ads that had men eating, none was eating "girl food."

Variation (repeat as many times as necessary): Consider women and men who challenge the norm of "girl food."

Example: While both men and women could classify a food as "girl food" or "guy food," three interviewees thought these norms were "absurd," "out-dated."

Interpretation: In American college culture, food is used as a means to make gender claims and also to resist gender norms. You can classify foods as foods that men are supposed to eat or women are supposed to eat. Images in the student newspaper support these classifications. But, a significant minority rejected these classifications, and used their rejection as a means to challenge and critique American gender norms. Specifically, they found food associations to be based on the American tendency to objectify both men and women.

Project Exercise 6
Group Conclusions and Future Research

****

Team Members:

Date:

Topic:

****

Instructions: *Using the format below (you may use more than the space provided, however), discuss your conclusions, limitations, future research, theoretical framework for future research, and justification for using that framework rather than others. All answers must be TYPED and in complete sentences. Also, everyone must turn in a team member assessment.*

Conclusions:

Contributions to Relevant Literature on Topic:

Limitations of Research Design:

Future Research:

Theoretical Framework for Future Research:

Justification for Using This Framework:

Project Exercise 7

Group Presentation

<u>**EVERYONE MUST TURN IN TEAM MEMBER ASSESSMENT, TOO.**</u>

****

<u>**Goal**</u>: To practice presenting research results in a professional conference presentation format.

<u>**Length**</u>: *15 min. Your group will be stopped after 15 min, and you will be graded only on the content you present. **BE SURE** to practice and time yourselves ahead of time.*

<u>**Content**</u>: The content for the presentation corresponds to and follows the project exercises. The following content must be covered and in the following order:

   I.   Group Topic—this can be your title slide
   II.   Overview of Trends in the Anthro Literature on That Topic
   III.   Research Goals and Aims
   IV.   Formative Theory
   V.   Basic Project Design
   VI.   Analysis: Themes and Subthemes With Examples From Transcripts and Fieldnotes; the Emergent Theory That Arose From Your Data Analysis That Explains the Themes, Subthemes, and the Relationships
   VII.   Conclusions
   VIII.   Limitations of Research Design
   IX.   Future Research

You will also turn in team member assessment on the day of your presentation.

<u>**Format**</u>: All groups are expected to use PowerPoint as a guide for the presentation. You are also expected to have an accompanying script.

- You will bring the presentation on a flash drive that will be plugged into the classroom computer. If you want to make sure there are no compatibility issues, bring the presentation by my office early. We will upload it to my desktop, which has the same software, and then save it to my work drive, which is accessible from the classroom.

<u>**Grading**</u>: You will get one group grade, which will then be multiplied for each team member by the average percentage participation derived from the team member assessments. The presentation grade will be based on three things:

1. *Coverage*—you will be assessed as to whether you covered the required components and how thoroughly you covered the components (see comments on graded exercises for guidance on how to be thorough).

2. *Clarity*—you will be assessed on how clear the presentation is. This includes the actual words in presentation and the delivery style.

3. *Format*—you will be assessed on how well the material is presented on the slides and the overall organization of the talk.

Some Important Notes:

1. Have everyone present at least one slide. Clearly, you will have more slides than group members. Select your clearest speaker who regularly participates in the group. Let her or him be your emcee.

2. Don't clutter the slides. This presentation is in conference presentation format. In a true conference presentation, you presume a level of familiarity with the information that allows you to put only the essentials on the slide. That is, you should put only the "take-away messages." Some people simply use a picture. This is OK, too, as long as you cover all the required components.

3. Practice, practice, practice. This is important to make sure you are within the time limit and that you have covered all key components.

4. One double-spaced page takes 2 minutes to read at a normal pace. That means you will have a seven, double-spaced page script. That's not much room. Select your words carefully to be able to cover the required materials sufficiently.

Project Exercise 8

Final Paper

****

<u>**Goal:**</u> To practice professional academic writing

<u>**ASSIGNMENT**</u>: Using your team's fieldnotes and interviews as well as your project exercises and presentation content, write a professional research article on your research project. Write the article using the formatting, style of writing, and organization detailed below.

<u>**LENGTH**</u>: Use no more than 3,000 words in body of text (this excludes title page and Works Cited page). This is approximately 10 to 12 pages.

<u>**FORMATTING:**</u>

TITLE PAGE: *Center the following text.*

Paper Title (bolded)

> Name

> Class

> Date

> Word Count

BODY OF ARTICLE

> 12 point font

> Double-spaced

> Standard margins

> Page number and initials at center of bottom of *each* page

> In-text referencing: *Every* time you use someone else's ideas, cite.

- If it's your words but someone else's idea, put (Last Name Year of Publication) at the end of the sentence, before the period.
- If citing actual words,
  - If it is no more than four lines, do not indent but put in quotes. At the end of the space, before the last period, put (Last Name Year of Publication: Page Number[s]).
  - If it is more than four lines, skip a line, indent, and single space. Before the last period, put (Last Name Year of Publication: Page Number[s]).

Anytime you use a quotation that is more than four lines long, indent and single-space it.

WORKS CITED PAGE: Use the following format.

Article

Last Name, First Name

Year   Title of Article. *Journal Name* Vol.(no.):page–page.

Book

Last Name, First Name

Year   *Title of Book.* Place of Publication: Publisher.

Book Chapter

Last Name, First Name

Year   Title of Chapter. *Book Name.* Eds., Last Name, First Name and Last Name, First Name. Place of Publication: Publisher. Page–page.

Writing:

The three MOST important things to remember about writing are

1. formal grammar,
   - no contractions, slang, abbreviations;
   - no ETC.;
   - spelling out numbers less than twenty;
   - no starting a sentence with numbers unless spelled out, regardless of amount;
   - no sarcasm, humor, or personal asides;
   - using "I" but only in reference to actions (e.g., "I used grounded theory analysis to identify themes and subthemes." But *not* "I think that the data imply"—we know you're writing it. You can just say "The data imply . . . "),

2. short, simple sentences and words (big words and five-line sentences only obscure your argument),
   - use this good rule of thumb, can an educated layperson understand the basic argument? If not, rewrite;
   - granted, there are some discipline-specific words (e.g., reification); if they are appropriate, then, by all means, use them,

3. getting it edited well before you turn it in. It is perfectly acceptable to have a friend read your paper for clarity and flow. The Writing Center can help with this, too. Note, however, no one, except your team members, are experts on the content or the methods employed—so, the editing is for readability, not content.

ORGANIZATION: Sections of body of article. **LABEL EACH SECTION WITHIN THE PAPER.**

Introduction: Give a summary of your research questions, methods, and why this is an important topic in social science. Then, write a paragraph that tells the reader exactly what you're going to do in this paper.

Literature Review: Justify your research question using existing literature. Does it answer a vexing question, apply an existing research question to a new population or setting, ask a new question about an old topic, or extend analysis of a research topic? Show what others have done, why this question needs to be asked, and how it will contribute.

Methods: This section must include a description of the topics used to guide data collection, actual methods used, and your method of analysis (in this case, grounded theory).

Results:

(Name of first theme)—discuss your first theme and how it helps to answer the research question. Include any subthemes. Be specific, detailed, and thorough with your evidence from fieldnotes and transcripts.

(Name of second theme)—discuss your second theme and how it helps to answer the research question. Include any subthemes. Be specific, detailed, and thorough with your evidence from fieldnotes and transcripts.

Continue with themes and subthemes until you have used all of them.

Discussion: In this section, tie together your themes to answer your research question and summarize your conclusions.

Limitations of research: Be very specific—here, you can include any group members dropping out, any issues with Participant Observation (PO) or interviews that you ran into, and any other practical problems. If relevant, also include a discussion of any problems with the topics you chose for PO or interviews. You will NOT be graded down for any practical problems you ran into—but you will be graded down if I don't know about them and see only limited data and analysis. So be sure to include them all!

Conclusion: Take your conclusions from the Discussion section and place it within the context of the larger relevant literature on the topic. Then, suggest future research directions based on this discussion, including theoretical, methodological, and topical changes you would make and/or add.

GLOSSARY[1]

The following terms are included in the exercises in this text. While you should use your textbook and class notes to elaborate, we have included brief definitions of these terms here for your reference.

Alpha Level. The probability of making a Type I error

Archival Data. Data from existing records (archives), generally analyzed qualitatively

Between Subject Design. A research procedure in which each member of the sample is randomly assigned to one attribute of the independent variable; the scores of the dependent variable are then compared

Bivariate Analysis. An analysis to determine the relationship between two, and only two, variables

Case Study. An in-depth analysis of one case (N = 1)

Cluster Sampling. A type of probability sampling in which the sample is divided into smaller groups (clusters) generally through random or **stratified sampling**. The sample is then chosen from each cluster

Coding. Assigning numerical (or other symbolic) codes to each attribute in a variable

Concept. An abstract idea that allows us to begin to understand and analyze the empirical world

Concept Map/Mapping. A graphical display of concepts, showing how they are interrelated

Conceptualization. Clearly defining the concept used in the research

---

[1]The definitions included here were compiled from a number of sources including the following:

- Babbie, E. (2001). *The practice of social research* (9th ed.). Belmont, CA: Wadsworth.
- Frankfort-Nachmias, C., & Nachmias, D. (2007). *Research methods in the social sciences* (7th ed.). New York: Worth.
- Nardi, P. M. (2006). *Doing survey research: A guide to quantitative methods* (2nd ed.). Boston: Allyn & Bacon.
- Vogt, W. P. (1999). *Dictionary of statistics and methodology* (2nd ed.). Thousand Oaks, CA: Sage.

Confidence Interval. A range of values around a population statistic that allows us to judge the accuracy of the boundaries of our sample statistic. Wider ranges will result in a larger confidence interval

Content Analysis. Analysis of human written, spoken or visual communications (newspapers, letters, magazines, webpages)

Continuous Variable. An interval or ratio level variables with a large number of numeric attributes that form a steady progression (e.g., 1, 1.1, 1.2, 1.3 . . .)

Control Group. The group that does not receive the treatment in an experiment

Correlation. An empirical relationship between two variables in which either the two variables are interrelated, or their attributes are interrelated

Cross Sectional Study. A study based on a cross section of population at a single point in time

Cross-Tab(ulation). A table showing the relationship between two or more variables, which shows all the attribute combinations

Degrees of Freedom. The number of values that are free to vary in a given statistical analysis

Dependent Variable. The variable that depends on, or is caused by, another, generally the independent variable

Descriptive Statistics. Statistics that summarize or describe variables

Dichotomous Variables. A nominal level variable with two attributes (e.g. male/female)

Double-Barreled Question. A problem in survey research question wording in which two ideas are combined into one question

Dummy Variables. A Dichotomous Variable generally coded 1 and 0 where 1 indicates the presence of an attribute and 0 indicates its absence

Endogenous Variable. A variable generated within the model. The variable's value is therefore determined by the model

Ethnography (Ethnographic Research). A qualitative method focusing on observation and participant observation; commonly used in anthropological research

Exhaustive. Response categories are considered exhaustive when a category is provided for all possible responses, and no subject is left unclassified

Experimental Group. The group that does receive the treatment in an experiment

Explanatory Variable. See Independent Variable

Extraneous Variable. A variable that is not part of a study that could have an effect on the dependent variable

Fieldnotes. Notes taken during ethnographic research

Focus Group. A type of group interview in which an interviewer asks a question of a group, and answers are given in open discussion

Frequency Distribution. A description of the number of times an attribute of a variable is observed in a sample

Generalizability. The ability to relate research findings to the larger population from a smaller sample

Hypothesis(es). A testable expectation about the relationship between two or more variables

Independent Samples *T* Test. A statistical test that compares the mean scores on a dependent variable for two independent groups

Independent Variable. The variable that is presumed to predict or explain the values of another variable, generally the dependent variable

Index. A set of items that combine to measure an underlying, shared concept

Inferential Statistics. Statistics that allow the researcher to make inferences about a population based on analysis of a sample

Likert Scale. A composite measure made up of standardized responses, such as strongly agree, agree, disagree, strongly disagree

Literature Review. A summary of past research

Longitudinal Study. A study designed to collect data over multiple points in time

Mean. An average computed by adding the values of all items in the data set (or subset) and dividing by the total number of items

Median. The middle score in a set of scores. Scores are put in order and the center is median.

Mode. The score that appears the most in a list of scores; the most common score.

Multicollinearity. When two or more variables are highly correlated and their individual effect on the dependent variables cannot be determined (used in Multiple Regression)

Multiple Regression Analysis. A statistical analysis that determines the impact of each independent variable on the dependent variable

Multivariate. An analysis to determine the relationship between multiple (more than two) variables

Mutually Exclusive. Response categories are considered mutually exclusive when each subject's responses fit into one and only one non-overlapping category

Null Hypothesis. A statement of no relationship between two variables

Operationalization. Specifies the exact way a variable will be measured; procedures involved in assigning values to the variables

Ordinal. A level of measurement in which attributes can be rank ordered

Outlier. A value of a variable that is extremely high or low when compared to the other values

Population. A group (generally of people but may also be organizations, artifacts, etc.) that the research will discuss through samples and generalizations

Prestige Bias. A problem in survey research question wording in which a highly respected group is linked to a response

Quantitative. Research and variables that are analyzed numerically

Random Sample. See Simple Random Sample

Regression. See Multiple Regression Analysis

Reliability. The consistency of a measure

Research. Systematic exploration of a topic that will describe or answer questions about a phenomenon

Research Design. The plan of collecting, analyzing, and interpreting data around a research question

Research Question. The question under investigation in the research

Research Topic. The topic under investigation in the research

Sample. A subset of cases drawn from a population; used to generalize to the population

Scale. A composite measure with order that is designed to measure a concept; a group of related measures of a variable (see Likert Scale)

Scholarly Research. Often referred to as *peer reviewed* research or primary research

Simple Random Sampling. A type of probability sampling in which each individual is chosen entirely by chance, but where each member has a known, non-zero, chance of selection; selection may be either with or without replacement

Skewed Distribution. A distribution of cases that is not normal (i.e., a bell-shaped curve); rather, the majority of cases are grouped at one extreme

Spurious Relationship. A relationship between two variables that is purely coincidental; while it appears as if two variables are related, the relationship is actually caused by a third variable

Standard Deviation. A measure indicating the distance between each score and the mean for a variable

Stratified Sampling. A type of probability sampling in which the population is first divided into strata; the sample is then randomly selected with members from each strata

Systematic Sampling. A type of probability sampling in which every Nth unit is selected. The Nth unit is generally randomly selected

T **Test.** A statistical test measuring whether the means of two groups are statistically different from each other

Test Statistic. Statistic used in determining statistical significance

Triangulation. The use of multiple research methods

Type I Error. The rejection of a null hypothesis that should have been accepted

Type II Error. The acceptance of a null hypothesis that should have been rejected

Unobtrusive Measures. Research that is conducted specifically such that the individual under observation is not aware that they are being studied.

Validity. The accuracy of a measure

Variable. Another that varies; a construct with multiple attributes

Within Subject Design. A research procedure in which each member of the sample takes on each attribute of the independent variable; each member changes on the dependent variable and is then compared

INDEX

$SAGE research methods online

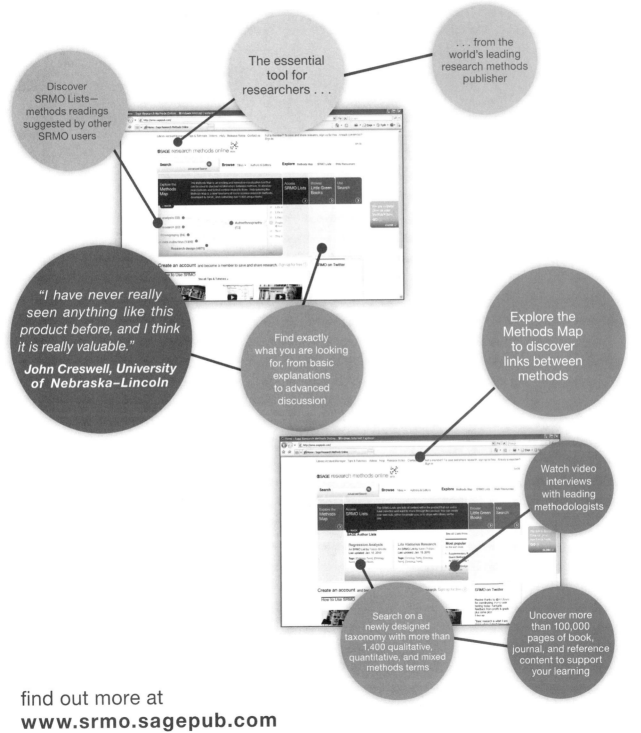

Discover SRMO Lists— methods readings suggested by other SRMO users

The essential tool for researchers . . .

. . . from the world's leading research methods publisher

"I have never really seen anything like this product before, and I think it is really valuable."

John Creswell, University of Nebraska–Lincoln

Find exactly what you are looking for, from basic explanations to advanced discussion

Explore the Methods Map to discover links between methods

Watch video interviews with leading methodologists

Search on a newly designed taxonomy with more than 1,400 qualitative, quantitative, and mixed methods terms

Uncover more than 100,000 pages of book, journal, and reference content to support your learning

find out more at
www.srmo.sagepub.com